Promoting Reflective Thinking in Teachers

CORWIN
PRESS

Promoting Reflective Thinking in Teachers

44
Action
Strategies

Germaine L. Taggart

Alfred P. Wilson

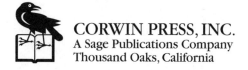

CORWIN PRESS, INC.
A Sage Publications Company
Thousand Oaks, California

For information:

Corwin Press, Inc.
A Sage Publications Company
2455 Teller Road
Thousand Oaks, California 91320
E-mail: order@corwinpress.com

SAGE Publications Ltd.
6 Bonhill Street
London EC2A 4PU
United Kingdom

SAGE Publications India Pvt. Ltd.
M-32 Market
Greater Kailash I
New Delhi 110 048 India

Printed in the United States of America

Library of Congress Cataloging-in-Publication Data

Taggart, Germaine L.
    Promoting reflective thinking in teachers: 44 action strategies /
by Germaine L. Taggart and Alfred P. Wilson.
    p.   cm.
    Includes bibliographical references and index.
    ISBN 0-8039-6712-8 (cloth: acid-free paper). — ISBN
0-8039-6713-6 (pbk.: acid-free paper)
    1. Teachers—Training of. 2. Teachers—In-service training.
3. Thought and thinking. 4. Teaching.   I. Wilson, Alfred P.
II. Title.
LB1707.T24 1998
370′.71—dc21   97-45382

This book is printed on acid-free paper.

98 99 00 01 02 10 9 8 7 6 5 4 3 2

Editorial Assistant: Kristen L. Gibson
Production Editor: Diana E. Axelsen
Production Assistant: Lynn Miyata
Typesetter/Designer: Rebecca Evans
Cover Designer: Susan Mathews

Contents

Preface

If change is to occur, reflective thinking must become a
taken-for-granted lens through which preservice teachers
conceptualize their practice.

—*Ross and Hannay (1986)*

Promoting Reflective Thinking in Teachers: 44 Action Strategies provides
teacher educators and staff developers, hereafter referred to as facilitators, with strategies to enhance the reflective thinking abilities of preservice and inservice educators. *Reflective thinking* refers to the process of
making informed and logical decisions, then assessing the consequences of those decisions. The guide was developed on the premise
that reflective thinking is required for effective teaching. Strategies for reflective thinking are approached at three levels: technical, contextual,
and dialectical. Within each level, strategies have been field-tested with
populations of preservice and inservice teachers. The guide has been reviewed by teacher educators across the nation to verify and validate its
usefulness.

Three major goals supported the construction of this document. One
was to develop a practical guide to be used by facilitators to augment the
reflective thinking of practitioners.

The second was to design a document that is nonlinear in nature. Information gleaned from teacher educators in a nationwide telephone
survey indicated the need for a guide with strategies that could be incorporated into existing course work as well as provide a general guideline
for staff development in a seminar or workshop format. The successful
use of this guide is not dependent on use in a lockstep, sequential fashion. The user is encouraged to select desired strategies that are pertinent
to the needs of particular practitioners.

A third goal is to provide several assessment strategies for facilitators
that would facilitate determination of a practitioner's reflective thinking
level so that a benchmark could be established and growth in reflective
thinking determined.

Each chapter focuses on a major component of enhancing reflective thinking of practitioners.

Organization of the Guide

Chapters are arranged with a logical progression in mind. Chapter 1 provides a basis for introducing reflective thinking to practitioners. A reflective thinking model is presented to show the cyclical nature of reflective thinking and to discern the steps of reflection. The process is graphically displayed as well as explained in writing. Three levels of reflective thinking—technical, contextual, and dialectical—are presented along with characteristics of practitioners who are functioning reflectively at each level. The chapter is intended to provide facilitators with background information regarding reflective thinking. Strategies and support materials may be used to provide background knowledge to practitioners on both the process and reflective levels.

A final section of Chapter 1 deals with preparing a plan of action for continued growth in reflective thinking. Joyce and Showers (1995) stress that learning activities should be extended over a period of time, with feedback and sessions spaced at intervals throughout the development process. A strategic plan of action will allow practitioners to use what has been learned about reflection to create a long-range plan that incorporates existing and newly acquired schemata and continual feedback. Through such a plan, the natural tendency of adults to problem solve and to resolve discrepancies between what is and what should be addressed can be enhanced.

The authors assume that when facilitating reflection, certain materials will be in place. An overhead projector should be in the session location as well as materials such as Vis-à-Vis pens, note cards, chart paper, newsprint, and masking tape. Many activities require clear transparencies to be used, as teams report information produced from their discussions. Other required materials have been kept to a minimum to enhance portability of the tasks. Facilitators may also opt to adapt guide materials to newer forms of technology, such as the use of computers and projection panels. Locations for sessions should support teaming activities. It is suggested that tables and chairs be used to provide a less formal structure than the traditional lecturer-audience room pattern.

Chapter 2 focuses on assessment of reflective thinking. Consideration of a practitioner's current reflective levels is paramount for providing individuals with benchmarks for determining reflective growth. An attribute profile is provided to be used in conjunction with other reflective thinking assessments to assist the facilitator and practitioners in determining levels of reflection. The use of the attribute profile will be one of the first activities used in course work and/or seminars. Practitioners should be assured that the profile is one component of many for obtaining baseline levels of reflection. There is no risk to taking the assessment. There are no correct or incorrect answers.

Strategies used to promote reflective thinking are the focus of Chapters 3 through 8. Strategies include observational learning; reflective journals; practicum activities, such as reflective teaching and microteaching; mental-model strategies, such as metaphors and repertory grids; narrative strategies, such as story, autobiographical sketches, and case study; and action research. For each strategy presented, an explanation is given along with reflective activities and questions. Action assignments, suggestions for success, journaling for reflective growth, and extended readings are provided to assist the facilitator in guiding practitioners through higher levels of reflective thinking. Strategies are intended to be selected based on general reflective levels of practitioners, interest levels of the practitioners, and the facilitator's knowledge of the skill levels of the practitioners. Not all of the strategies within each category are intended to be used during any one session. Strategies generally require little direct instruction by the facilitator. Teaming of practitioners to obtain a product for discussion, application of the product created, and promotion of discussion by the facilitator is essential.

Objectives for the facilitator provide focus as preparations are made toward presenting reflective thinking models, assessments, and strategies. Handouts and transparencies for each task are provided within each chapter.

Uses for the Guide

The intention of creating the reflective thinking guide was that it be used by staff developers as a resource from which to draw activities for seminars teaching reflective thinking strategies. It may also be used by teacher educators in university-based course work as a main or supplementary text to enhance reflection in preservice teachers.

The reflective thinking guide can be used by teacher educators in several ways. First, the guide may serve as the primary material for use in seminars or workshops to enhance the reflective thinking of practitioners. As a staff development guide, activities from the text may be selected to create a cohesive program 10 to 15 hours in length. As was stated earlier, to provide the practitioner with the most practice, reflection time, and meaningful feedback, it is recommended by the authors that the time frame be spread out over a 4-week to 6-week period, perhaps using five 3-hour sessions or four 4-hour sessions.

Second, the guide is designed for courses that correlate to participation of preservice teachers in field settings. When used in this context, activities found within the guide may be selected to support a particular experience or objective for each field experience. The activities may be incorporated in lessons focusing on such topics as classroom management or inclusion, leading the practitioners through a sequential process to being more reflective in their observations and practice.

Journaling is an important component of the reflective thinking process and should be encouraged by the facilitator. A variety of assessment techniques are also provided to assist in determining baseline reflective thinking levels and subsequent growth in reflective thinking.

Third, course work designed to prepare preservice teachers for imminent field experiences may provide a setting for use of the reflective thinking guide. Activities found in Chapter 1 may be used to introduce practitioners to the reflective thinking model and process. Also, activities such as "Observing Effective Questioning" and "Formatting a Journaling Entry" from Chapters 3 and 4, respectively, may be used to prepare practitioners for journaling or observational learning.

It is the sincere desire of the authors that this reflective thinking guide provide facilitators of preservice and inservice practitioners with an easy reference to strategies that fit the needs of both facilitators and practitioners. Attention is focused on portability in terms of time constraints and materials, value of strategies to promote increased reflection, and ease in selection of components to support existing course work and in providing tasks for seminars to enhance reflective thinking.

About the Authors

Germaine L. Taggart is Assistant Professor in the College of Education at Fort Hays State University, Hays, Kansas. She has taught students from kindergarten through grade twelve in public schools in Kansas. She received her BS and MS degrees in Elementary Education from Pittsburg State University, her EdS degree in Educational Administration from Fort Hays State University, and her EdD degree in Educational Administration from Kansas State University.

She teaches mathematics and science methods courses, has helped develop and continues to work with TEAM: Links for Learning (a field-based preservice program), and provides staff development on a consultant basis for school districts in western Kansas.

Dr. Taggart is married to Bruce R. Taggart. They have two children, Travis and Kelsey, and one granddaughter, MacKenzie. They reside at Hays, Kansas.

Alfred P. Wilson is Professor of Educational Administration at Kansas State University. He has served as a public school teacher and administrator and as a university faculty member and administrator in the states of Nevada, Utah, Montana, New Mexico, Idaho, and Kansas. He received his doctorate from Utah State University in 1969.

Author or coauthor of more than 25 books and monographs and 100 articles and research papers, he has been featured in three nationally distributed films. He has been consultant to more than 200 school districts in 42 states, 20 state departments and regional service centers for education, 15 community colleges and universities, and a broad variety of organizations.

Dr. Wilson has been an active member and leader in many organizations, including the American Research Association, Phi Delta Kappa, American Association of School Administrators, and the American Management Association.

1
Becoming a Reflective Teacher

An empowered teacher is a reflective decision maker who finds joy in learning and in investigating the teaching/learning process—one who views learning as construction and teaching as a facilitating process to enhance and enrich development.

—Fosnot (1989, p. xi)

Chapter Objectives

The facilitator will

Differentiate among the technical, contextual, and dialectical modes of reflective thinking

Recognize and be able to describe the cyclical process of reflective thinking

Be provided with tasks to help practitioners use the reflective thinking process

Be provided with tasks assisting in the recognition of characteristics of practitioners functioning in each of the three reflective thinking modes

Support preparation of a plan for continued growth in reflective thinking

R eflective thinking is the process of making informed and logical decisions on educational matters, then assessing the consequences of those decisions. Scholars of reflective thinking have grouped reflective thinking according to the mode of thinking or the process an individual progresses through to reach a level of reflection that complements both the context of the situation and the background the individual brings to the episode. This chapter will assist the facilitator with background knowledge for discussing both the modes and process of reflective thinking, tasks to use with practitioners desiring to enhance reflective thinking ability, and a format to aid practitioners in preparation of a plan for continued growth in reflective thinking.

Modes of Reflective Thinking

One way of manifesting the characteristics of reflective thinking is through modes of delivery. Scholars differ on the hierarchical nature of reflective thinking but generally agree on three modes or levels of reflective thinking: technical, contextual, and dialectical. The Reflective Thinking Pyramid provides an example of the three levels (Figure 1.1).

Technical Mode

Van Manen (1977) refers to the initial level of reflective thinking as *technical rationality*. Van Manen serves as a model for Lasley (1992) and Grimmett, MacKinnon, Erickson, and Riecken (1990) in that the first level of reflection deals with methodological problems and theory development to achieve objectives. Valli (1990) also refers to the first level as technical rationality but differs by positing that technical rationality is a nonreflective level. Valli's second level, practical decision making, adds reflection to the technical aspects of teaching.

Practitioners reflecting at the technical level function with minimal schema from which to draw when dealing with problems. Getting through lessons and using instructional management approaches are short-term measures that may be reflected on in terms of meeting outcomes. The individual, often isolated, episodes are building blocks for developing the professional repertoire needed to reflectively handle nonroutine problems. Many novice teachers are thought to function at a technical level based on a lack of schema in dealing with educative problems.

Outcomes for practitioners reflecting at a technical level may involve appropriate selection and implementation of lessons to achieve objectives. The objectives are not problematic nor does the practitioner deliberate on the context of the situation. Acquisition of skills and technical knowledge is important, as is methodological awareness and ability to implement a preset lesson. Technical practitioners may be

Dialectical Level

Addresses moral,
ethical or
socio-political issues;
disciplined inquiry;
individual autonomy;
self-understanding

Contextual Level

Looks at alternative practices;
choices based on knowledge
and value commitments;
content related to context/student needs;
analysis, clarification; validation of principles

Technical Level

Reference past experiences;
teacher competency toward meeting outcomes;
focus on behavior/content/skill;
simple, theoretical description

Reflective Thinking Pyramid

Figure 1.1. Reflective Thinking Pyramid

transitioning into linking theory development to practice and identification of the relevancy of activities and objectives. Practitioners need to be making observations and processing information to move toward solving problems and testing possible solutions for decision validity.

Facilitators working with practitioners functioning at a technical level should provide genuine, continuous experiences; observational learning instruction; and thoughtful discussion of problems and possible solutions. Experimentation and application of solutions with clear explanations and meaningful activities are also important. Sessions should provide necessary pedagogy, content, and theory and provide for use, examination, and analysis of instructional and management approaches. Knowledge of student characteristics will also be helpful to the technical practitioner in being able to reflect on problems faced in a field placement.

Contextual Mode

A second level of reflection (Grimmett et al., 1990; Lasley, 1992; Van Manen, 1977) involves reflections regarding clarification of underlying assumptions and predispositions of classroom practice as well as consequences of strategies used. The contextual mode deals with pedagogical matters as examined relative to a relationship between theory and practice. The nonproblematic nature of the technical level gives way to problems in the contextual level. Problems stem from personal biases resulting from a practitioner's belief system, looking at situations in context, and questioning of practices based on increased pedagogical knowledge and skills.

Outcomes for practitioners reflecting at this level may be understanding concepts, contexts, and theoretical bases for classroom practices, then defending those practices and articulating their relevance to student growth. Self-reflection to interpret and inform practice and establish congruency between theory and practice would be indicative of functioning at a contextual level. Clarification of assumptions and predispositions of practice and consequences helps contextual practitioners assess implications and consequences of actions and beliefs. Through increased practice and theoretical knowledge, practitioners examine competing views relative to consequences and actions and begin to develop routines and "rules of thumb." Understanding personal and environmental interactions is also a desired outcome for practitioners functioning at a contextual level.

Facilitators working with practitioners functioning at a contextual level should provide knowledge of situational constraints and external agents that may affect effective teaching. Time for collegial support, input, and discussion should be incorporated into sessions to provide bridges between and among concepts, theories, and practices. Questioning should be used to foster reflection with positive and timely feedback being provided.

Dialectical Mode

Van Manen's (1977) third and highest level of reflectivity, *critical reflectivity,* deals with questioning of moral and ethical issues related directly and indirectly to teaching practices. Critical reflectivity is comparable to the dialectical level of Grimmett et al. (1990) and Lasley (1992). At this level, practitioners contemplate ethical and political concerns relative to instructional planning and implementation. Equality, emancipation, caring, and justice are assessed in regard to curriculum planning. Practitioners are concerned with worth of knowledge and social circumstances useful to students without personal bias. The ability to make defensible choices and view an event with open-mindedness is also indicative of reflecting at a dialectical level.

Outcomes for practitioners functioning at the dialectical level relate to looking for and analyzing knowledge systems and theories in context and in relation to one another. Outcomes dealing with critical examination of underlying assumptions, norms, and rules; practicing introspection, open-mindedness, and intellectual responsibility (Dewey, 1933); and questioning moral and ethical issues of teaching, instructional planning, and implementation are all a part of higher aspects of reflection found at the dialectical level.

Concern with worth of knowledge and social consequence should be explored as well as defense of choices using external and internal dialogue. Classroom implications should be extended to society while reflecting on opposing viewpoints and cross-examining issues and practices. Risk taking on the part of the dialectical practitioner in the form of peer review and self-assessment independent of external standards or conditions will help the practitioner at this level achieve self-efficacy and self-actualization. Practitioners are developing expert knowledge and ability to reconstruct action situations as a means for reviewing self-as-teacher and questioning assumptions previously taken for granted. Examination of contradictions and systematic attempts to resolve issues are probable outcomes.

Facilitators working with practitioners functioning at a dialectical level should provide a forum to assist practitioners in deciding worthiness of actions and analyzing curriculum approaches, case studies, conventional wisdom, and technocratic approaches. Sessions should enable practitioners to look at issues in terms of optimum benefit for students and teacher empowerment. Action research should also be an outcome of reflective thinking at the dialectical level. Other activities may be analyzing stereotypes and biases through narratives and storytelling, practicing affective elements of caring and concern, and reflecting on the role of school climate and on society's role in education.

The Process Approach

Dewey (1933), Eby and Kujawa (1994), Pugach and Johnson (1990), and Schön (1983) delineate a cyclical process approach to reflective thinking. Figure 1.2 illustrates the reflective thinking process. In each instance, the first step to reflective thinking involves a problem. Dewey refers to such a problem as a "felt difficulty." Schön uses the term "problematic situation" as the initial step of reflection in action.

A second step in the process is to step back from the problem to look at the situation from a third-person perspective so that the problem may be framed or reframed (Clark, 1995; Pugach & Johnson, 1990; Schön, 1987). Dewey (1933) refers to the stage in which the problem is understood as one of providing location and definition. Eby and Kujawa (1994) dissect the process using components of observation, reflection, data gathering, and consideration of moral principles. These features provide the mental picture of the thought processes entertained by the reflective practitioner in an attempt to define a problem. Also represented at the definition stage are the parallel features of context and schema. The episode is likened to past events in an attempt to make sense of the problem and to search for possible solutions in the reflective thinker's repertoire. Once the reflective practitioner has searched for routine solutions to a possibly nonroutine situation or has devised possible solutions based on reasoning through similar past experiences, predictions are made and possible solutions generated. The solutions are systematically tested with subsequent observation and further experimentation, if needed, and judgments made relative to the level of success of the intervention. Dewey likened the process to the scientific method.

Evaluation, the next stage in the process, consists of a review of the implementation process and the consequences of the solution. Acceptance or rejection of the solution is made. If the solution proves successful, the instance may be stored for subsequent retrieval in similar situations or may become routine (Dewey, 1933). If the solution is not successful, the problem may be reframed and the process repeated.

Techniques for Facilitating Reflective Activities

A constructivist approach is used in this guide. Piaget (1975) was a proponent of the constructivist view of learning, which advocates learning as a process of change. Through simultaneous processes of assimilation and accommodation, new information is added to an existing repertoire of knowledge. *Assimilation* is a process by which knowledge is restructured so it can be integrated into existing schema. *Accommodation* is the process that allows practitioners to restructure knowledge by making modifications to existing schemata. When knowledge is constructed that correlates to existing schema, balance or equilibrium occurs.

Reflective Thinking Model

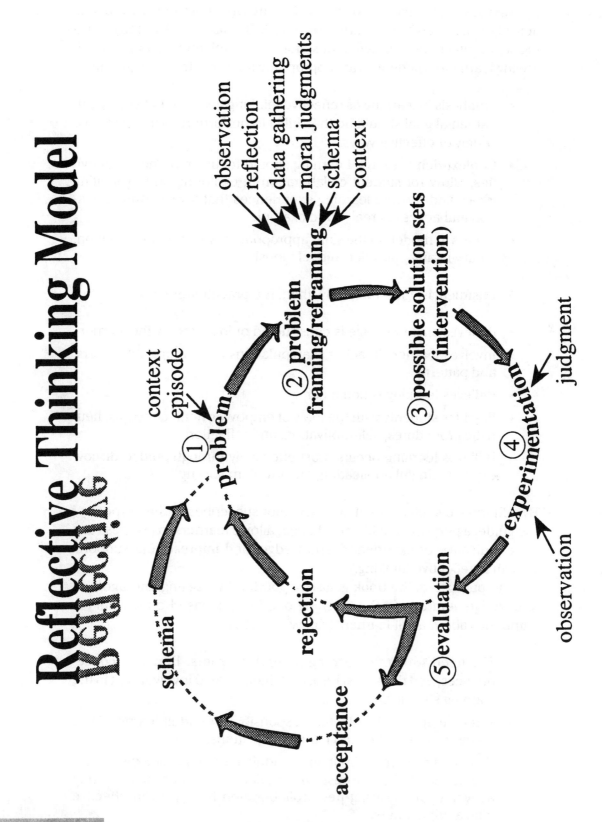

observation
reflection
data gathering
moral judgments
schema
context

context
episode

① problem

② problem
framing/reframing

③ possible solution sets
(intervention)

④ experimentation

judgment

observation

⑤ evaluation

rejection

acceptance

schema

Figure 1.2.   Reflective Thinking Model

Copyright 1996 by G. Taggart.

7

Two basic principles of constructivism are (a) what a person knows is actively assembled by the learner (Brooks & Brooks, 1993) and (b) learning serves an adaptive function of storage of useful information. The following learning experiences are appropriate for a constructivist program:

- Emphasis in learning as reflective thinking and productivity: A fundamental goal should be the ability to perform relevant tasks in a variety of effective ways.
- Context-rich learning: Learning should focus on authentic activities, allow for student collaboration in exploring and evaluating ideas, and provide learning experiences that foster communication and access to real-world examples.
- Access to models of the skills appropriate to the learning situation, ideally in an apprenticeship relationship

A constructivist (see Table 1.1), then, is a practitioner who

- Believes all knowledge is constructed or invented by the learner
- Involves learners in active manipulations of meanings, numbers, and patterns
- Believes learning is nonlinear
- Provides students with the tools of empowerment: concepts, heuristic procedures, self-motivation, and reflection
- Believes learning occurs most effectively through guided discovery, meaningful application, and problem solving

By adhering to such an ideal, the facilitator subscribes to the purpose of the guide, a purpose that fosters change; allows learners to progress at a pace indicative of experience, knowledge, and interest; and supports growth in reflective thinking.

The purpose of the book is also supported by existing andragogical knowledge. *Andragogy,* the teaching of adults, is based on several assumptions about adult learners (Knowles, 1990):

- The need to know is strong in adult learners. Benefits, consequences, and risks must be ascertained prior to involvement in the learning situation.
- Self-concept and intellectual responsibility of adult learners lend credence to self-directed learning situations.
- Experiential learning built on the adult learner's past experiences is essential. Group discussion, simulations, and problem-solving activities emphasizing peer collaboration have proven effective with adult learners.
- Readiness to learn is inherent in adult learners.

Table 1.1

A Constructivist . . .

- Believes all knowledge is constructed or invented by the learner

- Involves learners in active manipulations of meanings, numbers, and patterns

- Believes learning is nonlinear

- Provides students with tools of empowerment: concepts, heuristic procedures, self-motivation, and reflection

- Believes learning occurs most effectively through guided discovery, meaningful application, and problem solving

SOURCE: Adapted from *In Search of Understanding: The Case for the Contructivist Classroom.* By I. G. Brooks and M. G. Brooks, 1993, Alexandria, VA: Association for Supervision and Curriculum Development (excerpts). Used with permission.

- Connections to real-life situations and examination of relevancy issues motivate adult learners.
- Adult learners are often intrinsically motivated.

Responsibilities within the facilitative role of the staff developer or teacher educator that augment the andragogical model are such activities as presenting the relevance of ideas and concepts, allowing self-directed peer activities and the facilitation of discussion regarding those activities, and using knowledge of previous experiences or examination of existing schema on which to build current experiences. For these reasons, this guide has been constructed in a nonlinear fashion. A variety of activities for each topic and at each reflective thinking level have been created. Activities are often self-directed peer activities that allow the practitioners to construct their own knowledge, thus supporting intrinsic motivation and relevancy.

Certain techniques for facilitating learning have been supported by research and are used throughout the guide. What follows is a brief description of each technique to aid facilitators in role clarification.

Discussions

Classroom discussion is a basic teaching tool. *Classroom discussion* is defined in this guide as practitioners creating understanding by exchanging information, opinions, or experiences while working toward a common goal. The facilitator observes and encourages the group's efforts without becoming directly involved.

Grouping Practices

Grouping of practitioners will vary within the context of the activity objective. Whole-group discussion may be held as well as small team activities. Individuals will at times prepare a preliminary list of ideas for later discussion within a small team or whole group. Small team numbers will vary depending on the activity and are generally stated under the "Procedure" section of the activity. Also found in this section will be designated ways of sectioning teams and possible ways of determining team roles. Means for determining teams and roles should be considered as suggestions because factors such as group numbers and room logistics will affect partitioning of groups by the facilitator.

The facilitator's role within the group is to provide necessary background and directions, establish ground rules, present the assignment, and facilitate the work of the group in meeting the activity objective. Facilitation of an activity involves allowing practitioners to assume responsibility for the group's success. Do not interject your own ideas, opinions, or information. While practitioners are working in groups, move quietly about the room, monitoring but not interrupting. Show by your presence that you are supportive, attentive, and available. Encourage groups in difficulty by suggesting ways of problem solving rather than suggesting solutions.

Cooperative Learning

Cooperative learning is used widely today at all levels of education (Aronson, Blaney, Stephan, Sikes, & Snapp, 1978; Johnson, Johnson, & Holubec, 1991; Slavin, 1983). It is particularly effective for adult learners. Cooperative learning benefits learners by

- Increasing achievement through collaboration
- Improving relations among diverse learners (gender, age, culture, ethnicity)
- Developing problem-solving skills
- Fostering democratic processes in learning

Practitioners cooperate to complete the learning task. Cooperative learning tasks are set up in a manner where each participant has a role that must be adhered to if the task is to be completed. One example of cooperative learning tasks used in this guide is Task 12 (in Chapter 3), which uses the "jigsaw" technique (Aronson et al., 1978).

As the facilitator, your position is to promote group learning. The facilitator establishes purpose and rules, provides interesting and meaningful tasks, provides direction, and monitors group interaction. Assessment of task completion is necessary both from an academic standpoint and from a social standpoint. Not only must the task be completed well, but all members of the group must cooperate in its completion. Facilitators relate the value of working cooperatively to the practitioners.

Practitioners are expected to be self-directed and apply leadership techniques with the purpose of completing a task in a collaborative setting. They are responsible for the success of the team. Practitioners should be active, accountable, cooperative, and caring. Peer feedback and self-evaluation are important aspects of cooperative learning.

While monitoring cooperative groups, a facilitator needs to be mobile and observant. Groups are monitored for both academic success and social success. If intervention is needed within a team, enter the team at eye level, which promotes a sense of equality rather than superiority on the facilitator's part. Provide questioning that prompts the group returning to the task with the least amount of interference.

Brainstorming

Brainstorming will often be used during task discussions in this guide. A set time limit will be used, with practitioners expressing all the ideas on a given topic within time constraints. All answers are acceptable, the goal being quantity of ideas, uninhibited participation, and uncritical acceptance by team members. A recorder should be chosen prior to the brainstorming activity to write down the ideas of all other members. Questions used in brainstorming are generally literal and open-ended. Guidelines for brainstorming (see Table 1.2) are

- Preset time constraints
- Equality and democracy
- All ideas acceptable; be creative
- Volume of ideas important
- No discussion of ideas
- Risk-free environment
- Designated recorder

Consensus Building

Consensus building is a logical follow-up activity to brainstorming. After ideas have been generated, discussion is often necessary to decide what ideas best fit the current situation or question. The cardinal rule is that the solution must be acceptable by all team members. Consensus guidelines follow (Harrington-Macklin, 1994; see Table 1.3):

- Topic or idea is placed before the team for discussion.
- Topic is discussed, questions and concerns are raised, data and solution options are presented.
- Team decides whether to try to achieve consensus, how long it will spend, and what it will do if consensus cannot be reached.
- Differences and disagreements, as well as similarities, are explored and encouraged.
- Suggestions and modifications to the original topic are made.
- A new idea is created by the team on the basis of discussion.
- Facilitator checks for consensus.
- If no consensus, facilitator asks for a variation of the idea and tests for consensus again.
- If no consensus can be reached, facilitator suggests "stand aside" proposals (trial time period, modified plan).
- Facilitator tests consensus for stand-aside proposal.
- Facilitator tests for consensus to "stand aside" proposal.

Table 1.2 Guidelines for Brainstorming

- Preset time constraints
- Equality and democracy
- All ideas acceptable; be creative
- Volume of ideas important
- No discussion of ideas
- Risk-free environment
- Designated recorder

Promoting Reflective Thinking in Teachers: 44 Action Strategies
by G. L. Taggart and A. P. Wilson. Copyright © Corwin Press, 1998.

Table 1.3   Consensus Guidelines

- Topic or idea is placed before the team for discussion.

- Topic is discussed, questions and concerns raised, and data and solution options presented.

- Team decides whether to achieve consensus, the length of time to spend, and what to do if consensus cannot be reached.

- Differences and disagreements, as well as similarities, are explored and encouraged.

- Suggestions and modifications are made to original topic.

- Discussion by the team follows to create a new idea.

- Facilitator checks for consensus.

- If no consensus, facilitator asks for a variation of the idea and tests for consensus again.

- If no consensus, facilitator suggests "stand aside" proposals.

- Facilitator tests consensus for stand-aside proposal.

- Facilitator tests for consensus to "stand aside" proposal.

SOURCE: Adapted from Harrington-Macklin, 1994. Excerpted by permission of the publisher, from *The Team Building Tool Kit* by Deborah Harrington-Mackin. ©1994 New Directions Managment Services, Inc. Published by AMACOM, a division of American Management Association. http: www.amanet.org. All rights reserved.

Buzz Groups

Buzz groups are informal, loosely structured, and small. They are used to break down larger groups into smaller teams, which makes interaction of members less cumbersome. Buzz groups are generally practitioner run. Each team briefly addresses the problem at hand, records ideas, selects a designated reporter, then brings the team's ideas back to the whole group for presentation.

Role-Playing

Role-playing activities can help to improve understanding by allowing practitioners to think about and discuss the role of the speaker or writer, audience, or subject matter within a problem. The technique helps the facilitator gain insight into the feelings of the practitioners and in discovering what is important to them. Practitioners may be chosen or elect to participate in a particular role. The scenario is set by the facilitator, but the dialogue should be developed spontaneously. Discretion must be used to avoid embarrassment and discomfort.

Questioning

Effective questioning serves to meet several goals (Heathcote, 1980). Through effective questioning, the facilitator may

- Bring focus to an activity
- Cause group members to reflect on alternatives not otherwise discussed
- Promote identification of issues in more depth
- Control the direction or mood of the practitioners
- Promote beliefs and values clarification
- Deepen insight of practitioners

Heathcote also suggests several guidelines for questioning: Effective questions must be real; help practitioners focus on where they are, what they are doing, and why; lead practitioners to wonder about and seek out new information; and move practitioners to reflect on the significance of actions.

There are many kinds of questions. Among them are

- Information-seeking questions
- Questions that encourage research
- Questions that supply information
- Questions that require group decision making
- Class-controlling questions

- Questions that establish mood and feeling
- Questions that foster beliefs and values
- Questions that foster insight

Activities for Introducing Reflective Thinking to Practitioners

The following activities will assist the facilitator of reflective practitioners with introducing reflective thinking. Activities involve formulating a definition of reflective thinking and using the reflective thinking model to enhance reflective thinking on the part of practitioners. By analyzing the model and illustrating the use of the process, practitioners should correlate the benefits of its use with problems in their own lives.

The first meeting with practitioners should be for the purpose of reviewing the model, as it is the central element of most of the tasks in this chapter. Activities are set up to facilitate ease of use. A topic and objective are provided along with a materials list and time constraints. The procedure for each task is systematically simple. Little preparation is needed after material gathering and reading for background knowledge has been completed. A description of several techniques used in the procedure section of each activity is found on previous pages in this chapter. Evaluations support the task objective. Debriefing questions are questions that should promote reflective thinking of practitioners at the conclusion of the activity, generally in a whole-group situation.

Task 1   Finding a Definition

Topic: Defining Reflective Thinking

Objective: Participants will devise and revise a definition for reflective thinking by writing an initial definition, sharing first with a colleague, then with the group, and finally reaching a consensus on one definition.

Materials: Chart paper or newsprint; masking tape; Post-it notes; Prominent Reflective Thinking Definitions (Table 1.4); Consensus Guidelines (Table 1.3)

Time: 30 minutes

Procedure:
1. Inform practitioners that to assess growth in reflective thinking, it is necessary to reach consensus on a definition. Distribute and review Consensus Guidelines.

2. Invite practitioners to write individual definitions of reflective thinking. Allow approximately 5 minutes.

3. Pair practitioners by allowing them to choose a peer with whom they have a high comfort level. Between the two, consensus must be reached and a second definition written on chart paper. Each pair should have the second definition written, hung in a visible location, and be prepared to discuss within 5 minutes.

4. Distribute one Post-it note to each practitioner. Instruct practitioners to vote by placing their Post-it note on the definition that most reflects their own thinking.

5. Discuss as a whole group why the majority definition was selected.

6. Distribute Prominent Reflective Thinking Definitions to practitioners. Compare group definition with researched definitions.

Evaluation: Participants' definition should have three commonalities found in most "expert" definitions: methodical process, inquiry orientation, and change or self-improvement as a goal.

Debriefing:
1. Was the individual definition easy to write? What made it easy? Difficult?

2. How were the paired partners able to reach consensus on a definition?

3. For what reason did you vote for a particular definition?

4. Why is it important to create a definition indicative of the practitioner?

5. How did the group's definition compare to the experts' definitions?

6. Were there commonalities among all definitions?

Promoting Reflective Thinking in Teachers: 44 Action Strategies
by G. L. Taggart and A. P. Wilson. Copyright © Corwin Press, 1998.

Table 1.4   Prominent Reflective Thinking Definitions

Bigge and Shermis (1992)	Reflective learning is problem raising and problem solving. Fact-gathering is combined with deductive processes to construct, elaborate and test hypothesis.
Brubacher, Case, and Reagan (1994, p. 36)	[Reflective thinking is] our attempts to understand and make sense of the world.
Dewey (1933, p. 9)	[Reflective thinking is] active, persistent, and careful consideration of a belief or supposed form of knowledge in the light of the grounds that support it and the further conclusions to which it tends.
Lasley (1992, p. 24)	Reflection . . . refers to the capacity of a teacher to think creatively, imaginatively and at times, self-critically about classroom practice
Norton (1994, p. 139)	[Reflective thinking is] a disciplined inquiry into the motives, methods, materials and consequences of educational practice. It enables practitioners to thoughtfully examine conditions and attitudes which impede or enhance student achievement.
Ross (1989, p. 22)	[Reflective thinking is] a way of thinking about educational matters that involves the ability to make rational choices and to assume responsibility for those choices.
Ross and Hannay (1986)	[Reflective thinking is] a process involving decision-making in a socio-political context, identification of problems, a search for satisfactory answers, and investigation of social problems realized in living.
Schön, (1983, p. 151)	It [the cycle of inquiry] is initiated by the perception of something troubling or promising, and it is determined by the production of changes one finds on the whole satisfactory or by the discovery of new features which give the situation new meaning and change the nature of questions to be explored

Promoting Reflective Thinking in Teachers: 44 Action Strategies
by G. L. Taggart and A. P. Wilson. Copyright © Corwin Press, 1998.

Task 2   The Reflective Thinking Process

Topic: The Reflective Thinking Model

Objective: The practitioner will review the reflective thinking model, then present a scenario showing the components of the model through role-playing.

Materials: Overhead transparency of Reflective Thinking Model (Figure 1.2); "Can't Sit Still" Scenario (Table 1.5), one copy per each participant—write or type on the bottom of each copy one of the following so that there is an even distribution of each:

> Twinkle, Twinkle Little Star
> Row, Row, Row Your Boat
> Mary Had a Little Lamb
> Itsy, Bitsy Spider
> Old MacDonald

Time: 1 Hour

Procedure: 1. Present the model of reflective thinking to practitioners by using the Reflective Thinking Model. Discuss the cyclical nature of the model using the background information presented earlier in this chapter.

2. Distribute "Can't Sit Still" scenarios to practitioners. Have them read them silently. Discuss the facts within the scenario as they relate to the reflective thinking model.

   Problem: Danny's excessive movement
   Frame-reframe: Arthritis causes need for movement
   Possible solution sets or intervention: Cardboard office
   Experimentation: Use of cardboard office

Evaluation: To be decided

Acceptance or rejection: To be decided

3. Group participants into five teams by referring them to the bottom of the scenario sheets, where you have written one of the earlier-mentioned children's song titles. Practitioners are to hum the tune of the song assigned to each of them as they navigate about the room listening for others humming the same tune. The last individual to enter the team is the leader.

Promoting Reflective Thinking in Teachers: 44 Action Strategies
by G. L. Taggart and A. P. Wilson. Copyright © Corwin Press, 1998. *continued*

Task 2   Continued

4. Practitioners are to create a brief scenario to role-play for the whole group that depicts the reflective thinking model. Review role-playing rules. Allow 15 minutes for preparation.

5. Each team will present their role-play to the whole group. Immediately after each presentation, hold a brief discussion of the model components relative to the role-playing scenario. The overhead transparency of the model may be helpful in discussing the components.

Evaluation: Scenarios used in role-play should reflect components of the reflective thinking model.

Debriefing: 1. Does the model fully represent the process of reflective thinking?

2. Is one component more important than another?

3. Can you think of other scenarios that follow the reflective thinking model? Explain.

4. How might this model relate to journaling situations?

Table 1.5 "Can't Sit Still" Scenario

For the fourth time that morning, Danny had to be told to return to his seat, and once again, he returned to what he had been doing within a few minutes. His morning was spent dancing with the full-sized skeleton, looking out the window, picking on other students, and lying on the floor or his desk. "If I have to warn you again," said the teacher," you will visit the principal to discuss your problem!"

"But I wasn't doing anything!" Danny shouted, as he threw his pencil into the air.

"Write your name in the book," demanded the teacher.

Danny had been having problems all year. Because Danny has arthritis, he has two desks, which allows him to move from desk to desk whenever he feels the need. The problem is that he takes this privilege too far.

Danny has never been tested for a learning disability. He does attend a special reading class once a day. The remainder of his day is spent in the regular classroom.

"Today, we are going to try something different," the teacher said as she walked to the back of the room. "I have an office that I want you to try." She set a large cardboard partition on Danny's desk. "Let's see if this helps you stay on task," she added.

Danny's mother is aware of Danny's problems at school. She visits with the teacher at least once a week. Danny also is required to take home daily assignment sheets. If there is a stamp on the sheet, Danny had a good day. Danny has a deal with his mother. If he brings home a certain number of good slips, she will take him to a basketball game.

Promoting Reflective Thinking in Teachers: 44 Action Strategies
by G. L. Taggart and A. P. Wilson. Copyright © Corwin Press, 1998.

Task 3   Gardening Puzzle

Topic: Introduction of the Reflective Thinking Model

Objective: The practitioner will use the Reflective Thinking Model to devise a plan for partitioning a garden plot equitably among four individuals.

Materials: Reflective Thinking Model (Figure 1.2); copies of the Garden Plot Problem (Figure 1.3); Garden Plot Solution (Figure 1.4); colored pencils

Time: 20 minutes

Procedure: 1. Prior to the beginning of the session, use colored pencils to outline the garden plot on Garden Plot Problem copies. Use one color on two sheets, then a second on the next two sheets, and so on until all garden plots are color coded.

2. Group participants into pairs by the color coding on each person's Garden Plot Problem sheet.

3. Once participants are paired, allow 10 minutes for participants to process through the reflective thinking model to find a plausible solution to the problem:

Four friends have recently purchased a garden plot in the shape shown. They want to divide it into four individual gardens the same shape and size. Help them solve their dilemma.

4. Call on a practitioner to demonstrate the solution on the overhead project. Using the Garden Plot Solution, discuss the model and solutions.

Evaluation: Check for reasonable solutions that fit the criteria.

Debriefing: 1. Did the reflective thinking model provide a process for problem resolution?

2. Was reframing necessary?

3. What did each participant bring to the problem?

Promoting Reflective Thinking in Teachers: 44 Action Strategies
by G. L. Taggart and A. P. Wilson. Copyright © Corwin Press, 1998.

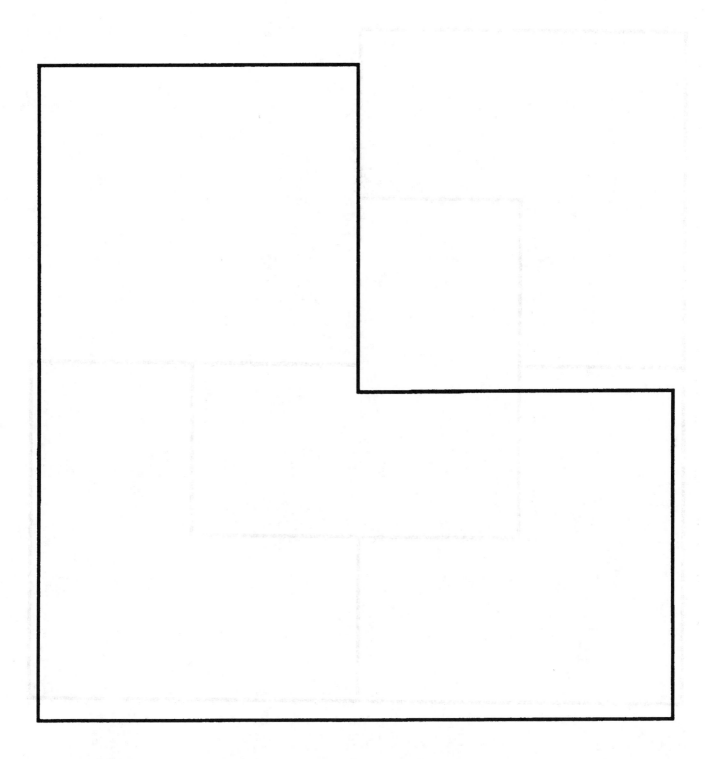

Four friends have recently purchased a garden plot in the shape shown. They want to divide it into four individual gardens the same shape and size. Help them solve their dilemma.

Figure 1.3. Garden Plot Problem

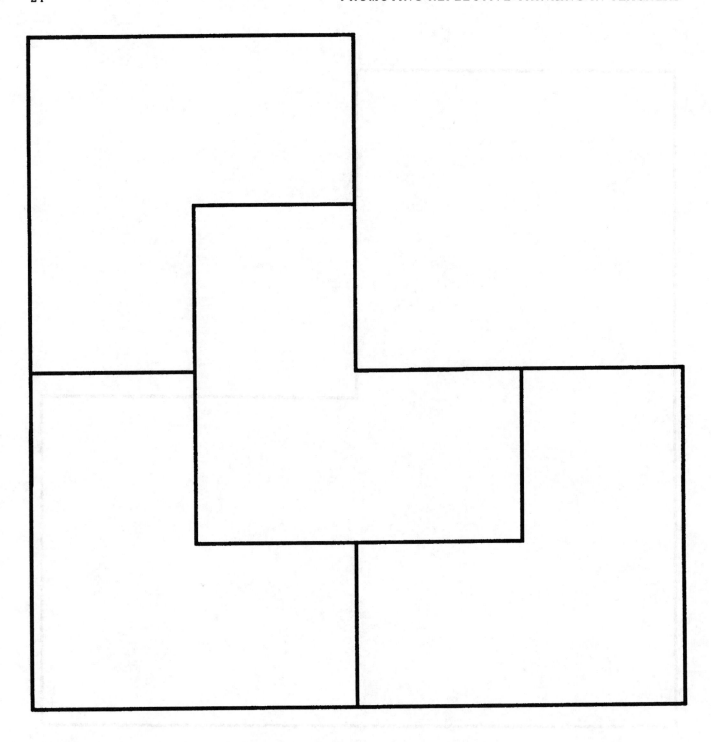

Figure 1.4. Garden Plot Solution

Promoting Reflective Thinking in Teachers: 44 Action Strategies
by G. L. Taggart and A. P. Wilson. Copyright © Corwin Press, 1998.

Task 4 Roll On

Topic: Introduction of the Reflective Thinking Model

Objective: The practitioner will use the Reflective Thinking Model to demonstrate the process of reflective thinking by devising possible solutions to the "roll on" dilemma.

Materials: Reflective Thinking Model (Figure 1.2); toilet paper rolls (enough for every team of three to have a unique design or color); Consensus Guidelines (Table 1.3)

Time: 20 minutes

Procedure: 1. Group participants by randomly distributing individual sections of various designs or colors of toilet paper.

2. Provide each team with a roll of toilet paper, and pose the following problem:

   Some individuals place toilet paper on the roller so that the end of the roll comes over the top toward the front; others prefer the end to dangle from the bottom at the back of the roll. If you are wanting the end sheet at its most accessible point, what is your group's preference for placement of the roll on the toilet paper roller? Justify your answer.

3. Once participants are grouped, allow 10 minutes for participants to process through the Reflective Thinking Model reaching consensus, then clarifying and justifying the team's position.

4. Randomly call team leaders (shortest person on the team) to explain the team's position.

Evaluation: Check for reasonableness of solutions and justification.

Debriefing: 1. Consensus is an agreement by all participants on an issue. How was your team able to reach consensus?

2. Did the reflective thinking model provide a process for problem resolution?

3. Was reframing necessary?

4. What type of experimentation was necessary?

Promoting Reflective Thinking in Teachers: 44 Action Strategies
by G. L. Taggart and A. P. Wilson. Copyright © Corwin Press, 1998.

Task 5   Designing a Classroom

Topic: Introduction of the Reflective Thinking Model

Objective: The practitioners will use the Reflective Thinking Model to devise a physical plan of a classroom housing 40 students that would accommodate team teaching by two teachers.

Materials: A deck of playing cards; Reflective Thinking Model (Figure 1.2); Classroom Layout (Figures 1.5A & 1.5B); Consensus Guidelines (Table 1.3)

Time: 40 minutes

Procedure: 1. Group participants in quartets by randomly distributing playing cards (an Ace, King, Queen, Jack, etc.) to each participant.

2. Provide each team with a copy of the Classroom Layout and present scenario.

   Devise a physical plan of a classroom housing 40 students that would accommodate team teaching by two teachers.

   Scale is 1 cm = 4 ft. Each student desk is 2 ft long and 1½ ft wide. Teacher desks are 4 ft × 2 ft. Room size and layout is indicated on Classroom Layout sheets.

3. Once participants are grouped, allow 20 minutes for participants to process through the reflective thinking model, reach consensus on a layout, sketch it onto the grid paper, and develop justification for the solution.

4. Randomly call on team leader (person who has attended college the longest period of time) to present layout and justification.

Evaluation: Check for reasonableness of solutions and justification.

Debriefing: 1. Consensus is agreement by all participants on an issue. How was your team able to reach consensus?

2. Did the reflective thinking model provide a process for problem resolution?

3. What experiences were brought into the discussion?

4. How did the team evaluate the solution?

Figure 1.5A. Classroom Layout

☐T☐ = Teacher's Desk   ◼S◼ = Student's Desk
                        (4' x 2 ')   (2' x 1 1/2 ')

Figure 1.5B. Classroom Furniture

NOTE: 1 cm = 4 ft.

Task 6 Logic Lure

Topic: Introduction of the Reflective Thinking Model

Objective: The practitioner will use the Reflective Thinking Model to devise a plan for getting all characters in the dilemma to the opposite side of the river.

Materials: Reflective Thinking Model (Figure 1.2); Logic Lure (Figures) transparency (Figure 1.6—characters should be shaded or colored and cut out to allow for mobility when demonstrating the process); Logic Lure (Scene; see Figure 1.7)

Time: 20 minutes

Procedure: 1. Group participants into pairs, counting off by the number that when multiplied by two will equal the number of total practitioners.

2. Once practitioners are grouped, allow 10 minutes for them to process through the reflective thinking to find a plausible solution to the problem that follows:

   A boy owned a dog, a rabbit, and a bag of vegetables. One day, he was on the edge of a gorge, where there was a shaky old swinging bridge that was only strong and wide enough to hold him and one of his possessions. If he left the dog and rabbit alone, the dog would eat the rabbit. If he left the rabbit and the vegetables alone, the rabbit would eat the vegetables. How did he get safely across the gorge with all three of his possessions?

Evaluation: Check for reasonable solutions that fit the criteria.

Debriefing: 1. Did the reflective thinking model provide a process for problem resolution?

2. Was reframing necessary?

3. What did each participant bring to the problem?

Figure 1.6. Logic Lure (Figures)

SOURCE: Maridith Bouchey. Used with permission.

Logic Lure

Dog, Rabbit, and a Bag of Vegetables

A boy owned a dog, a rabbit and a bag of vegetables. One day he was on the edge of a gorge, where there was a shaky old swinging bridge that was only strong and wide enough to hold him and one of his possessions. If he left the dog and rabbit alone, the dog would eat the rabbit. If he left the rabbit and the vegetables alone, the rabbit would eat the vegetables. How did he get safely across the gorge with all three of his possessions.

Maridith Bouchey 2/98

Figure 1.7. Logic Lure (Scene)

SOURCE: Maridith Bouchey. Used with permission.

Preparing a Plan of Action for Enhancing Reflective Thinking

In discussing enhancing reflective thinking on the part of practitioners, Dewey (1933) recommends three attitudes that must be nurtured: open-mindedness, whole-heartedness, and intellectual responsibility. *Open-mindedness* refers to an intellectual receptiveness to alternatives. *Whole-heartedness* requires a mental, emotional, and physical commitment to solving problems on the part of practitioners. Reflective practitioners then consider intellectual responsibility toward long-term and short-term solutions to the problem.

Development of a plan to evaluate change is the final step toward enhancement of reflective thinking. The purpose of this step is threefold. First, practitioners examine the degree to which their plan is workable given the constraints of the field setting and the degree to which those constraints can be overcome or can preclude the intervention's implementation. Second, systematic monitoring of how well the plan is being adhered to must be done. Self-evaluating and self-monitoring encourages and reinforces reflection on changes in teaching performance. Last, practitioners develop an evaluation plan to determine the effectiveness of the change. The facilitator provides a foundation and encourages practitioners to implement and follow the planning strategy and models, planning for evaluation as needed.

If the plan of action is successful, the practitioner has created a new understanding and reached a higher level of reflection. If the plan of action is unsuccessful, the practitioner continues the cycle of inquiry and reflection, taking into consideration the new information resulting from unsuccessful experimentation toward reaching a goal. Thus, the cycle parallels the reflective thinking model.

During a final 1-hour or 2-hour experience, whether it be in short sessions with preservice practitioners or at the end of a seminar experience, allow practitioners time to develop a plan of action for future growth in reflective thinking. Practitioners will develop one or two specific goals. For each goal, a list of strategies will be made that support reaching the goal. Strategies may include those incorporated throughout the guide, or practitioners may want to select particular strategies indicative of a focus area of concern. Each strategy should be outlined in terms of tasks for completion; target completion dates; and necessary materials, input, and knowledge to complete the task.

Monitoring of the goal's achievement should be formative as well as summative. Identifying those constraints that may serve to block achievement of the goal is essential. Identification of those support resources that will serve to augment goal achievement is equally essential. Devise a monitoring strategy. Establish how feedback will be collected and evaluated. Also, establish definitive criteria for determining that a goal has been met. Most important, plan for success, and plan to celebrate success. Communicate to others your achievements. Tables 1.6 and 1.7 may be used to provide a basic structure on which to create a plan to enhance reflective thinking.

Table 1.6 Preparing a Plan of Action

- Strategy
- Tasks for completion
- Target completion date
- Necessary materials
- Input
- Knowledge needed to complete the task
- Monetary considerations
- Constraints
- Suggested resources
- Collection of information and feedback
- Evaluation and feedback

Table 1.7 Plan of Action: Enhancement of Reflective Thinking

Goal

Strategy	Tasks	Completion Date	Support Materials	Constraints	Monitoring Method and Criteria	Method of Calibration

Assessing Reflective Thinking

It is more important to make teachers thoughtful and alert students of education than it is to help them get immediate proficiency.

—*Dewey, 1933*

Chapter Objectives

The facilitator will

Determine a baseline level of reflection

Assess personal and practitioner growth in reflective thinking

Understand the attributes that are indicative of reflective practitioners

Determine a level of reflection in writing

T he benefits of reflective thinking are great. But how do you know
where an individual functions as a reflective practitioner? How can
you establish a baseline so that growth in reflection can be assessed?
What constitutes evidence of reflection?

Little has been done to systematically assess reflective thinking. In
fact, some proponents of reflective thinking contend that assessment in
any quantifiable form is invalid (Ross, 1990) because the reflective thinking process is incapable of being observed and because agreement on a
definition of reflective thinking has not yet been ascertained (Hattan &
Smith, 1994). Zeichner and Liston (1987) followed preservice teachers
into their professional careers to continue monitoring reflective growth.
Kirby and Teddlie (1989) and Cruickshank (1985) also measured reflective thinking of practitioners at a technical level. Program effectiveness
was studied by Korthagen (1985), Korthagen and Wubbels (1991), Ross
(1989), and Sparks-Langer, Colton, Pasch, and Starko (1991). Little can be
generalized from these evaluation attempts because the "means for
gathering and analyzing data pose a considerable challenge for researchers, for it is difficult to establish unequivocally that reflection has taken
place" (Hattan & Smith, 1994, p. 5).

Evaluative efforts have often been qualitative in nature, studying the
impact of reflective thinking at the preservice level. Qualitative research
allows the researcher to view development of reflection in context. The
use of preservice teachers provides a manageable population in size and
setting. Such studies provide only isolated reports of program success or
growth in reflective levels (Zeichner, 1987).

Several teacher educators have researched ways to analyze and code
writing samples of practitioners (Hattan & Smith, 1995; Ross, 1990; Simmons & Sparks, 1987). Written assignments, such as journaling, autobiographical sketches and narratives, are ways of recording reflective
thought. Concerns were voiced, however, as to the ability of those
thoughts to be translated into reflective action.

Sparks-Langer et al. (1991) provide three orientations to reflective
thinking of practitioners: cognitive, critical, and narrative. The cognitive
approach emphasizes decision making based on information gathering
and processing. Problem framing using ethical and moral reasoning is
the focus of the critical approach. Teacher experiences, values, sociopolitical implications, and goals form benchmarks for decision making.
The critical approach uses personal narratives, naturalistic inquiry, case
studies, and action research to focus on circumstances under which decision making takes place.

Eastern Michigan University was the setting for Sparks-Langer et al.'s
(1991) studies on reflective thinking of preservice teachers. A framework
(see Table 2.1) for measuring and describing reflective thinking types
was developed to show "a growing sophistication of teachers' schemata
. . . from technical concepts and rules to contextual and ethical thinking"
(p. 7). The framework shows seven levels of reflection. The first level

indicates no descriptive language and the second, simple layperson description. Little if any reflection takes place at these two levels. At levels three and four, events labeled with appropriate terms and explanation, with tradition or personal preference given as the rationale, respectively, are indicative of the technical mode of reflective thinking. At levels five and six, explanation with principle or theory given as the rationale and explanation with principle or theory and consideration of context factors, respectively, are indicative of practitioners functioning at a contextual level. Level seven shows characteristics of practitioners functioning at the dialectical level as explanations with consideration of ethical, moral, and political issues are presented.

Table 2.1   Framework for Reflective Thinking

Level	*Description*
1	No descriptive language
2	Simple, layperson description
3	Events labeled with appropriate terms
4	Explanation with tradition or personal preference given as the rationale
5	Explanation with principle or theory given as the rationale
6	Explanation with principle or theory and consideration of context factors
7	Explanation with consideration of ethical, moral, political issues

SOURCE: Sparks-Langer et al., 1991, p. 26; reprinted by permission.

Hattan and Smith (1995) assessed the process of reflection in an attempt to identify evidence of reflection. The focus was on defining characteristics of individuals' writing. Four writing styles and defining criteria were developed and tested. The first, *descriptive writing,* was not considered reflective as only a description was present with no attempt made to provide rationale or take issue with an event. The second set of characteristics was termed *descriptive reflection.* Criteria included justification in addition to description, often based on experience. The third writing style, labeled *dialogic reflection,* was written in third person with judgments, exploration of reasoning, and recognition of multiple perspectives. *Critical reflection,* the fourth writing style, has the individual responding to episodes by relating to influences of multiple historical and sociopolitical contexts.

In looking for other criteria for assessment of reflective thinking, Noordhoff and Kleinfeld (1990) looked at videotaping episodes followed by conferencing with practitioners as a way to reflect on teaching purpose and methodology. Though time-consuming and, at the preservice level, often a contrived teaching experience, Noordhoff and Kleinfeld contend that teaching behavior and judgment can be assessed using videotaping. Their experience in rural Alaska shows that preservice teachers, through microteaching assessments, could move from viewing teaching as task oriented to viewing the teaching experience as a problematic act dependent on contextual factors—designating growth from the technical level of reflection to the contextual level. Rubric construction provides a way to analyze effective teaching. Narratives reflecting on the microteaching experience and evaluated using criteria from the Reflective Thinking Pyramid (Figure 1.1) provides a means for determining level of reflection for teaching actions.

The Reflective Thinking Pyramid, by definition, builds progressively from a basic general premise to a peak of reflection epitomized by individual autonomy and self-understanding. The base of the pyramid is a technical level where knowledge is derived from human experience as well as pedagogy, content, and methodology of education. Practitioners bring to the educational experience past histories and knowledge gleaned from content, skills, and behavior observations to produce reflective individuals capable of meeting set outcomes, learning theory to support a skill base, and making simple, rational observations. The technical level is evidenced in the writing of practitioners who

- Make simple descriptions of observations
- Focus on behaviors, content, and skills from past experiences or theory derived from readings or course work, without looking for alternatives
- Are task oriented, viewing teaching competency as meeting a set of objectives

- Use appropriate educational vocabulary to correspond with current skill and pedagogy level

Practitioners reflecting at the contextual level of the pyramid have progressed to a comfort level evidenced by a willingness to look for alternative approaches that best fit the needs of the students and the context of the situation, choices based on knowledge and value commitments and analysis, clarification, and validation of principles found in teaching. The contextual level is evidenced in the writing of practitioners who

- Reflect on practices as those practices affect students' learning
- Reflect on decisions relative to the context of the situation
- Relate theory to practice
- Focus on action
- Look for alternatives to practice based on knowledge and personal values
- Analyze, clarify, and validate practices based on sound teaching constructs

Practitioners reflecting at the dialectical level of the pyramid have progressed to an autonomous state evidenced by disciplined inquiry, reflection-in-action, self-actualization, and an open-mindedness that allow them to address moral, ethical, and sociopolitical issues in teaching. The dialectical level is evidenced in the writing of practitioners who

- Systematically question practices
- Suggest alternatives and competing theories
- Reflect on decisions and consequences during the course of the action
- Bring moral, ethical, and sociopolitical issues to bear on educational practices
- Express themselves verbally and in their writing with efficacy and self-confidence

Several researchers have explored the correlation among reflective thinking and various attributes associated with effective practitioners. LaBoskey's study (as cited in Copeland, Birmingham, De La Cruz, & Lewin, 1993) investigated a connection between reflectivity and a proactive nature. Zeichner and Liston (1987) suggested that teachers' value systems are related to reflectivity. Wubbels and Korthagen (1990) indicated that reflective teachers have an openness to innovation and that relationships with students and colleagues were more favorable with higher levels of reflective thinking. Improvement in teaching (Bolin, 1988; Munby & Russell, 1989) and heightened connections between theory and practice were evident in reflective educators (Cruickshank, 1985).

A collective list of teacher attributes (see Table 2.2) from the research, which are believed to be evidence of reflective thinking, provides a core for the Profile of Reflective Thinking Attributes (Form 2.1). The profile, not meant to be a quantitative diagnostic tool of reflective thinking in and of itself, is to be given to practitioners at the onset of sessions on reflective thinking. There are no right or wrong answers. No stigma should be placed on presence within any level. The instrument is designed to be one of several tools used in triangulation of data to assess an approximate baseline level of reflection so that growth may be determined. "Triangulation is the act of bringing more than one source of data to bear on a single point" (Marshall & Rossman, 1995, p. 144). Data from a variety of sources corroborate and elaborate the findings. Analogous to this concept are the quantitative tools, such as blood pressure instruments or thermometers, with which a physician collects information to get a more holistic picture of the health of a patient.

Table 2.2 Reflective Thinking Attributes

Reflective practitioners . . .

Identify and analyze problems and situations

Look at problems relative to educational, social, and ethical issues

Critically consider contextual and pedagogical factors

Use a rational problem-solving approach

Make intuitive, creative interpretations and judgments

Are metacognitively, analytically, and instructionally skillful

Possess self-efficacy, intrinsic motivation, and a desire for lifelong learning

Are open to experimentation and new innovations

Have job satisfaction

Make decisions consciously and tentatively

View situations from multiple perspectives

Set personal short-term and long-term goals

Plan and monitor actions, then evaluate results of those actions

Have essential skills for attaining and using information

Correct understandings of concepts underlying facts, procedures, and skills

Consider general characteristics of so-called best practice

Are flexible in a search for alternative explanations

Use evidence in supporting or evaluating a decision or position

Have a commitment to values (e.g., all students can learn)

Have a strong commitment to systematic and rational reflective thinking

Show responsiveness to educational needs of students

Question personal aims and actions

Constantly review instructional goals, methods, and materials

Are a proactive force in education

Are intellectually perceptive to multiple and novel ideas

Are committed to problem resolution (whole-heartedness)

Commit adequate resources to reflective thinking (time and physical, mental, and emotional energy)

Welcome peer review, critique and advice

Write (journal) events reflectively

Adapted from Dewey, 1933; LaBoskey as cited in Copeland, Birmingham, De La Cruz, and Lewin, 1993; Ross, 1989; Schön, 1987; Simmons and Sparks, 1987; Sparks-Langer et al., 1991.

Form 2.1 Profile of Reflective Thinking Attributes

To explore your current level of reflective thinking, respond to the following questions. For each statement, circle the number of the indicator that best reflects your agreement:

4 = Almost always
3 = On a regular basis
2 = Situational
1 = Seldom

When confronted with a problem situation,

1.	I can identify a problem situation	4	3	2	1
2.	I analyze a problem based upon the needs of the student	4	3	2	1
3.	I seek evidence which supports or refutes my decision	4	3	2	1
4.	I view problem situations in an ethical context	4	3	2	1
5.	I use an organized approach to problem solving	4	3	2	1
6.	I am intuitive in making judgments	4	3	2	1
7.	I creatively interpret situations	4	3	2	1
8.	My actions vary with the context of the situation	4	3	2	1
9.	I feel most comfortable with a set routine	4	3	2	1
10.	I have strong commitment to values (e.g., all students can learn)	4	3	2	1
11.	I am responsive to the educational needs of students	4	3	2	1
12.	I review my personal aims and actions	4	3	2	1
13.	I am flexible in my thinking	4	3	2	1
14.	I have a questioning nature	4	3	2	1
15.	I welcome peer review of my actions	4	3	2	1

 continued

Form 2.1 Continued

When preparing, implementing, and assessing a lesson,

16.	Innovative ideas are often used	4	3	2	1
17.	My focus is on the objective of the lesson	4	3	2	1
18.	There is no one best approach to teaching	4	3	2	1
19.	I have the skills necessary to be a successful teacher	4	3	2	1
20.	I have the content necessary to be a successful teacher	4	3	2	1
21.	I consciously modify my teaching to meet student needs	4	3	2	1
22.	I complete tasks adequately	4	3	2	1
23.	I understand concepts, underlying facts, procedures, & skills	4	3	2	1
24.	I consider the social implications of so-called best practice	4	3	2	1
25.	I set long-term goals	4	3	2	1
26.	I self-monitor my teaching	4	3	2	1
27.	I evaluate my teaching effectiveness	4	3	2	1
28.	My students meet my instructional objective when evaluated	4	3	2	1
29.	I use a journal regularly	4	3	2	1
30.	I engage in action research	4	3	2	1

Tally the number of the circled indicators, write the number of each tally below, multiply by the indicator number, then total each of the subtotals to reach an overall score.

Indicator 4 × _____ = _____

Indicator 3 × _____ = _____

Indicator 2 × _____ = _____

Indicator 1 × _____ = _____

Total _____

Practitioners mark the Profile of Reflective Thinking Attributes instrument, tally the number of circled indicators, place the numbers on the line after the appropriate indicator on the second page, then multiply the indicator by the tally number to arrive at a subtotal. Add the four subtotals together and write the score in the space indicated. Use the following scale of totals to determine an appropriate level of reflection.

Technical level   = Below 75

Contextual level = 75 to 104

Dialectical level = 105 to 120

Provide for discussion following the use of this instrument. Here are some possible debriefing questions:

- What level(s) of reflection was (were) most evident? Why do you suppose this level was most prevalent?
- Which of the attributes do you consider to be the most indicative of a reflective practitioner?
- How might the information gleaned from completing this profile help you in achieving growth of reflective thinking?

Using the "Attribute Clarification" or "Card Sort: Reflective Thinking Attributes" activities in this chapter will support the use of the Profile of Reflective Thinking Attributes and assist practitioners in defining a reflective practitioner. Stress to practitioners that this is only one indication that provides them with a baseline level of reflection. There are no right or wrong answers. No stigma should be attached to reflection level.

The following activities may be used after practitioners have completed the Profile of Reflective Thinking Attributes. The activities are intended to validate the attributes found in the profile and clarify reflective thinking and levels of reflection.

Task 7   Attribute Clarification

Topic: Attributes of reflective thinking practitioners

Objective: Practitioners will use the attributes found in the Profile of Reflective Thinking Attributes to create possible examples or actions derived from possession of the attributes.

Materials: Profile of Reflective Thinking Attributes (Form 2.1); three sheets of chart paper or newsprint placed about the room on which 10 profile statements have been written so that teams may write examples of each attribute under the corresponding attribute; watercolor markers

Time: 45 minutes

Procedure: 1. Allow 5 minutes for practitioners to respond to the Profile of Reflective Thinking Attributes. Collect.

2. Group practitioners into teams by age groups of students taught either in field experience or in their own classrooms. Be sure teams are manageable in numbers—split teams of more than five practitioners. Allow for no single-practitioner groups.

3. Instruct practitioners to review 10 of the items on the profile. Designate which 10 items (i.e., 1-10; 11-20; or 21-30) each team will discuss. This may be done arbitrarily, but work to be sure each set of items has an equal number of teams reviewing it. Teams are to briefly discuss each item, then create two or three possible examples or actions derived from possession of the attributes. Allow 10 minutes for discussion at the end of which practitioners will have written their examples under the appropriate profile item on the chart paper spaced around the room.

4. After the first set of 10 attributes is reviewed, move teams clockwise to the next set of 10 items. Allow 10 minutes for practitioners to write additional examples or actions using watercolor markers to existing ones on the chart. Move teams a third time and repeat the process with the last set of items.

5. Discuss the types of examples and actions that practitioners have determined indicative of each attribute.

continued

Task 7   Continued

Evaluation: Practitioners should have collectively provided 8 to 10 examples or actions indicative of each attribute.

Debriefing: 1. Were there attributes that prompted a higher degree of knowledge? experience?

2. Were there attributes that were found more readily in the actions of team members? Less readily?

3. Which attributes indicate a higher level of reflection on the part of the practitioner?

4. Are there attributes not on the list that you feel should be included?

Task 8   Card Sort: Reflective Thinking Attributes

Topic: Attributes of reflective practitioners

Objective: Practitioners will analyze attributes indicative of reflective practitioners then self-evaluate their possession of these attributes.

Materials: Profile of Reflective Thinking Attributes (Form 2.1); Attribute Cards (Table 2.3) xeroxed on six different colors of paper then laminated and cut apart; Category Cards (Table 2.4) photocopied, laminated and cut apart; overhead transparency of Reflective Thinking Pyramid (Figure 1.1)

Time: 30 minutes

Procedure: 1. Allow 5 minutes for practitioners to respond to the Profile of Reflective Thinking Attributes. Collect.

2. Group practitioners by distributing one of each of the six colors of cards randomly to each participant so that six equal teams are formed. Give each team the remainder of the cards that match the color of cards team members have collected (i.e., all green cards form a team; all reds, etc.).

3. Explain to practitioners that the cards contain attributes of effective teaching. Participants are to sort cards into three categories. The first category, labeled "Technical," will house those attributes that apply to practitioners who bring to the educational experience knowledge gleaned from content, skills, and behavior observations. Focus is on a competency level that allows practitioners to meet a set of predetermined objectives. A second, labeled "Contextual," will represent attributes of teachers who look for alternative approaches that best fit the needs of students and the context of the situation. A third column, "Dialectical," will reflect cards dealing with attributes of teachers who function at a critical thinking level that addresses issues of morals, values, and sociopolitical issues. Each attribute card can be placed in only one column. Allow 15 minutes.

4. Instruct teams to discuss the rationale for placement of attribute cards into the corresponding category. Teams should also discuss individuals' self-evaluation of possession of these attributes.

5. Discuss the Reflective Thinking Pyramid and its use in assessing reflection.

Promoting Reflective Thinking in Teachers: 44 Action Strategies
by G. L. Taggart and A. P. Wilson. Copyright © Corwin Press, 1998   *continued*

Task 8   Continued

Evaluation: Practitioners will sort attribute cards according to category, then self-evaluate possession of attributes.

Debriefing: 1. Are reflective practitioners effective practitioners? Provide rationale for your answer.

2. Could some of the attribute cards fit into other categories? Why do you think so?

3. Where do you believe reflection begins? How can you tell if you are reflective?

4. Was there a particular category in which most practitioners found themselves?

Table 2.3   Attribute Cards

Identifies and analyzes problem-solving situations	Uses a rational problem approach
Looks at problems relative to educational social and ethical issues	Critically considers contextual and pedagogical factors
Makes creative interpretations and judgments	Has job satisfaction
Is metacognitively, analytically, and instructively intuitive	Views situations from multiple perspectives

Possesses self-efficacy, intrinsic motivation, and a desire for lifelong learning	Sets personal short-term and long-term goals
Is open to experimentation and new innovations	Makes decisions consciously and tentatively
Plans, monitors, then evaluates actions	Searches for alternative results
Has essential skills for attaining concepts and using information	Corrects under-standings of under-lying facts, proced-ures, and skills
Considers general characteristics of so-called best practice	Questions personal aims and actions

Uses evidence in supporting or evaluating a decision or position	Has a commitment to values (e.g., all students can learn)
Has a strong commitment to systematic and rational reflective thinking	Is a proactive force in education
Shows responsiveness to educational and instructional needs of students	Constantly reviews goals, methods, and materials
Is intellectually perceptive to multiple and novel ideas	Possesses flexibility in thinking

Is committed to problem resolution (whole-heartedness)	Writes (journals) events reflectively
Commits adequate resources to reflective thinking (time and mental, physical, and emotional energy)	Welcomes peer review, critique, and advice
Commits to reaching objectives	Implements discipline system
Is task oriented	Focuses on lesson design and implementation

Table 2.4   Category Cards

Technical	Contextual
Dialectical	

Practicing Observational Learning

Observational learning is theoretically conceptualized as a skill that can be developed along a learning hierarchy from acquisition and fluency to generalization of initiative behavior.

—*Browder, Schoen, and Lentz (1986-87, p. 447)*

Chapter Objectives

The facilitator will

Assist practitioners in demonstrating proficiency in the use of the observational strategy

Be able to assess growth in reflective thinking on application of the strategy

Analyze personal competence of the strategy to assist practitioners in preparing action plans that will foster personal reflection on return to the classroom situation

Facilitate maintenance of reflective journals to be used by practitioners for personal growth assessment and for peer assessment

T eacher educators who support the concept of reflective thinking use several strategies that provide input and modeling coupled with experiences to develop metacognitive skills. These skills and experiences may also enhance reflective thinking of practitioners (Bullough, 1991; Connelly & Clandinin, 1986; Hattan & Smith, 1995; Korthagen, 1985; Sparks-Langer et al., 1991). Among those strategies found to be most effective and functional with practitioners are observational learning; journaling; narratives; practicum techniques; mental processes, such as metaphors and repertory grids; and inquiry-oriented processes. Throughout the remainder of this book, these mentioned strategies will be discussed; uses at the technical, contextual, and dialectical levels will be provided; and follow-up activities suggested. Chapter 3 deals with the enhancement of observational skills to bring about growth in reflective thinking.

The Observation Process

Bandura (1968) defines observational learning as one's ability to acquire new responses by observing the behavior of a model. Much of what is learned in education is through observation. Observation is a skill that practitioners must possess to develop insights needed to make wise decisions. Observations should be ongoing, systematic, and developed to the point that a focus can be established, notes taken, and actions explored in a relatively short amount of time with high effectiveness. Inferences and judgments are not components of the observation process, which makes the observation skill difficult for many practitioners, especially novices. According to McHaney and Impey (1992), judgmental statements are generally nonspecific and undefined, whereas descriptive statements are specifically defined. Examples follow:

Judgmental: The child responded well to questioning.

Descriptive: The child responded correctly to five out of six questions.

Techniques that facilitate observation in novice practitioners are the determination of a single focus, setting minimum time constraints, and developing criteria and instrumentation to make collection of observational data easier to accomplish. As practitioners become more skilled, scripting in the form of narratives, anecdotal records, running records, and visual mapping may be possible, providing for "thick" descriptions likened to the information-laden documents of ethnographers. Narratives are open-ended, low-structured descriptions of events. Anecdotal records differ from narratives as a particular event is described with detail. Two parts of anecdotal records are facts and interpretations of facts.

Running records are kept on the occurrences of an observational objective over a period of time and without judgment or interpretation. Visual mapping is a way of using images of an observation rather than words. Seating charts or drawings of room arrangements are forms of visual mapping.

Instruments of observation should be easy to use and readily adapted for a variety of purposes and time constraints. Rating scales (Borich, 1994) provide simple instruments for recording behavior as well as the degree to which behaviors occur. Examples are checklists and Likert scales. Checklists tend to be more subjective, whereas Likert scales are often objective, incorporating judgment and interpretation on the part of the observer. Other instruments may be designed to allow observers to tally occurrences of a particular event.

Experience with observational practice brings opportunity for more complex foci, longer time limits, and flexibility in criteria and instrumentation.

Possible foci for observations are

- Individual behaviors
- Lesson structure
- Attitudes toward technology
- Roles of teachers
- Classroom management effectiveness
- Teaching techniques
- Student response to teaching techniques
- Relationships between and among practitioners, students, and so on

Observations may be made as participant observers or nonparticipant observers. As participant observers, duties within the classroom are simultaneously carried out along with the observation process. Nonparticipant observers are "looking in" on the action, taking a third-person point of view. In either instance, the practitioner engages in attempts to understand perceptions through indicators such as overt behaviors, verbal expressions, or subtle body language.

Browder et al. (1986-87) suggest that observational skills are developed at three levels: *acquisition,* imitation of a discrete model; *fluency,* imitation of complex functional behaviors with greater independence; and *generalization,* imitation of behavior of a withdrawn model. This hierarchy can aid in determining level of observational skills, recognizing essential variables in planning, and organizing instruction that will enhance the practitioner's ability to acquire more complex behaviors.

According to Borich (1994), observation learning plans should be developed and revised for self-improvement at a level that matches one's own stage of experience. Borich also lists eight goals of observation:

1. To achieve empathy
2. To establish cooperative relationships
3. To become realistic
4. To establish direction
5. To attain confidence
6. To release enthusiasm
7. To become flexible
8. To become self-reliant

Systematic observational learning

- Encourages view of practitioner as a flexible decision maker
- Fosters a realistic view of teaching as a profession
- Allows focus on specific skills
- Allows practitioners to relate better to students
- Fosters higher levels of comfort within the classroom for practitioners
- Allows practitioners time to view teaching behaviors modeled by others
- Permits practitioners to observe parallels of teaching behaviors and student learning behaviors
- Provides common vernacular
- Fosters self-improvement

Learning is not only dependent on what we see but how those observations are processed. Separating dialogue from observation is not conducive to developing shared understandings of educative practice (Clarke, 1995). Dialogue between and among practitioners and facilitators provides a forum for the sorting out of facts and interpretations and for working through the problem-solving process. Facts and interpretations may be looked at more critically. Multiple perspectives are brought to bear on the observational situation.

Debriefing questions built into the activities presented in this chapter are intended for use in a collaborative environment. The facilitator is to foster discussion of observation to analyze, clarify, and evaluate the learning environment. Activities are written at each of the three reflective levels: technical, contextual, and dialectical. Activity selection should be based on the experiences of practitioners and levels of reflection determined by using the Profile of Reflective Thinking Attributes (Form 2.1).

Reflective Activities

Technical Level

At a technical level, practitioners generally have not had many experiences on which to formulate solutions to problematic classroom situations. The following two activities, "Categorization of Observations" (Task 9) and "Compliance with Classroom Rules" (Task 10), will assist practitioners in building nonjudgmental observations, creating simple instruments for recording observations, and interpreting data collected from observations.

Task 9   Categorization of Observations

Topic: Observational learning

Objective: The practitioner will prepare a list of classroom observations, then categorize them according to "Roles in the Classroom," "Classroom Environment," "Communication," and "Professionalism."

Materials: Clear transparencies; markers; four newsprint charts placed about the room, labeled "Roles in the Classroom," "Classroom Environment," "Communication," and "Professionalism"

Time: 30 minutes

Procedure: 1. Instruct practitioners to individually observe the current classroom setting for 5 minutes, listing observations on a piece of note paper. During the observation period, provide a variety of short activities for participants, such as discussing room arrangement, summarizing activities to this point in the session, asking for points of clarification from practitioners, and so on. As a facilitator, be mobile; vary your voice tone, volume, and inflection; use proximity; dress professionally; and use educational terminology.

2. Divide practitioners into groups of four or five based on shoe color. The individual on each team driving the greatest distance to the session will be the leader. The individual driving the shortest distance will be the recorder.

3. Teams are to collectively analyze the lists of each individual according to the topics, "Roles in the Classroom," "Classroom Environment," "Communication," and "Professionalism." The observations are then to be placed on the corresponding topic sheet hanging about the room. If the item already appears on the newsprint list, there is no need to repeat it. Allow 15 minutes for discussion and transfer of lists by the recorders.

4. Select the leaders of four of the teams to each summarize one of the newsprint lists. Input derived from team discussion may be obtained from the leaders as well as members of the whole group. The aim is to, in turn, discuss how each item fits under one of the categories.

                    continued

Task 9   Continued

Evaluation: Practitioners will have observed the classroom setting, compiled a list of observations, and collectively categorized the observations.

Debriefing: 1. What other categories might be appropriate for placement of some of your observations?

2. Did any of your observations not fit one of the categories? Were there observations that could fit more than one category?

3. Did inferences enter into your observations? If so, what might be the effect of allowing inferences to alter actual observations?

4. What might be other observational strategies for recording the information observed?

Task 10   Compliance With Classroom Rules

Topic: Observational learning

Objective: The practitioner will create an observation instrument, then use it while observing the current classroom environment and assessing the number of students who comply with all classroom rules throughout a preset 15-minute period.

Materials: Clear transparencies (two for facilitator and one for each team); transparency of Observation Instrument (Table 3.1) and enough copies for teams of three participants

Time: Two 20-minute periods; one 15-minute classroom observation

Procedure: Day 1

1. Ask practitioners to briefly discuss possible classroom rules with an individual near them, then list them on a sheet of paper. Allow 5 minutes.

2. During whole-group discussion, reach consensus on four or five rules typically found in a classroom setting. Stress that rules are to be stated in a positive manner. Write the rules on a clear transparency placed on the overhead projector.

3. Discuss a possible format that would allow practitioners to reach the objective. Possible alternatives are tally sheets, rating scales, or checklists. Each would indicate the classroom rules and means for marking the observed behaviors. Show transparency of Observation Instrument (Table 3.1). Add rules suggested by practitioners and possible adaptations to reach objectives.

4. Distribute individual copies of the Observation Instrument and assign a revision of the instrument to meet the needs of the practitioners. Practitioners may work in pairs or trios based on grade or age level of classroom assignments. Fifteen minutes of observation are to be made in a current classroom environment. Practitioners are to record the number of students who comply with classroom rules throughout that time period using the instrument designed.

   NOTE: Variations to the instrument may be

   a. Separate columns for males and females

   b. Specific area to record comments regarding actions of those who are not complying with rules

   c. Simultaneous use of the instrument during the same classroom episode by two observers, with later comparisons made

continued

Task 10 ——— Continued

Day 2

1. Practitioners will be teamed in the same pairs or trios formed to create the observation instrument. Each team will elect a leader. Allow 5 minutes for teams to collect thoughts on the value of the instrument created and used in recording desired data. Provide each team with a transparency on which to sketch their instrument.

2. Call on the leaders of each team in turn to briefly explain to the whole group their instrument and its value. Encourage practitioners to use the overhead and the sketch of the instrument to facilitate understanding the team's efforts.

Evaluation: Creation of an instrument that focuses on observation of students complying with classroom rules

Debriefing: 1. What are suggested ways of adapting the instrument to meet the practitioners' needs?

2. Are other topics suitable for observations? What might they be?

3. Why is it important to record only observable behaviors?

4. At what point are practitioners' inferences justifiable?

5. How might data collected from an observation instrument be used?

Table 3.1   Observation Instrument

Classroom Rules	

Contextual Level

Practitioners reflecting at a contextual level should make up the majority of the group. They are able to analyze problems according to context, incorporating theory within practice and addressing the needs of students. The following two activities will assist practitioners in making observations of more complex situations, amending instruments to fit context, and interpreting data collected from observations.

Task 11   Observing Effective Questioning

Topic: Observational learning

Objective: The practitioner will use an observational rating system to assess questioning effectiveness in a classroom situation.

Materials: Individual copies of Questioning Strategies (Table 3.2); clear transparencies (two for facilitator and one for each team); individual copies of Observational Checklist for Effective Questioning Strategies (Table 3.3); deck of playing cards

Time: Two 30-minute periods; one 15-minute classroom observation period

Procedure: **Day 1**

1. Distribute copies of Questioning Strategies. Discuss with practitioners questioning strategies that have been proven to be effective based on research findings.

2. Group practitioners into quartets by randomly distributing playing cards (Ace, King, Queen, Jack, etc.) to each participant.

3. Distribute a copy of Observational Checklist: Effective Questioning Strategies to each team. Allow 15 minutes for teams to discuss and amend the checklists to reflect classroom teaching assignments.

4. Instruct practitioners to use the Observational Checklist for a 15-minute observation period in individual's field setting.

Day 2

1. Practitioners will be teamed in the same trios formed during the Day 1 activity. Each team will elect a leader. Allow 10 minutes for teams to collect thoughts on the value of the instrument created and used in recording desired data. Provide each team with a transparency on which to sketch their instrument.

2. Call on the leaders of each team in turn to briefly explain to the whole group their instrument and its value in determining questioning effectiveness in the classroom.

                    continued

Task 11   Continued

Evaluation: Use of an observational rating system to assess questioning effectiveness in a classroom setting and the analysis of the instrument's use through group discussion

Debriefing: 1. What are suggested ways of adapting the instrument to meet the practitioners' needs?

2. What needs prompted changes made in the instrument prior to use?

3. Why is it important to record only observable behaviors?

4. At what point are practitioners' inferences justifiable?

5. How might data collected from an observation instrument be used?

6. What might be advantages to using a checklist? Disadvantages?

Table 3.2   Questioning Strategies

- State questions briefly and clearly

- Ask one question at a time

- Provide at least 3 seconds wait time

- Use a variety of questions

- Sequence questions

- Use higher-order questions

- Provide positive feedback

- Provide cues, if needed

- Encourage students to ask questions

- Require a response

Table 3.3 Observation Checklist for Effective Questioning Strategies

Questioning Strategy	Check If Observed
State questions briefly and clearly	_____
Ask one question at a time	_____
Provide at least 3 seconds wait time	_____
Use a variety of questions	_____
Sequence questions	_____
Use higher-order questions	_____
Provide positive feedback	_____
Provide cues, if needed	_____
Encourage students to ask questions	_____
Require a response	_____

Task 12   Observing Classroom Management Styles

Topic: Observational learning

Objective: The practitioner will use a narrative format while observing a current classroom environment to distinguish individual classroom management styles as being low, moderate, or high teacher control environments.

Materials: Definition: Classroom Management (Table 3.4); Synopsis of Classroom Management Styles (Table 3.5); individual copies of Classroom Management Approaches (Table 3.6); Classroom Management Chart (Table 3.7), one copy per each team of three; clear transparencies

Time: One 45-minute period; one 15-minute classroom observation period; one 25-minute period

Procedure: *Day 1*

1. Discuss with the whole group the definition of classroom management. Ask for factors that have helped to determine practitioners' management styles. List factors as presented on clear transparency. Distribute and review briefly the Classroom Management Approaches hand-out to provide an overview of models to be discussed.

2. Group participants into teams of three by having them count off to whatever number multiplied by three will equal the total number of practitioners. Within each team, members will become experts on either low, moderate, or high teacher control environments. The tallest team member will become an expert at low control environments, the shortest team member will become an expert at high control environments, and the remaining team member will become an expert at moderate control environments.

3. Practitioners will use a modified version of JIGSAW (Aronson, Blaney, Stephan, Sikes, & Snapp, 1978), a strategy designed for processing divergent information. Practitioners from different teams who have corresponding environmental control topics form temporary groups called "expert groups." Each expert group meets to assist its members in discussing the characteristics and approaches of their corresponding environmental control topic. Distribute Synopsis of Classroom Management Styles for the expert groups to use as information and to prompt discussion of possible examples. Allow about 15 minutes.

continued

Task 12   Continued

4. "Experts" return to original teams to discuss the levels of environmental control within classroom management styles with team members using the additional information and examples supplied by the expert groups. Allow 15 minutes.

5. Bring the whole group together to discuss management styles and examples considered by each team and to answer any questions that may have developed.

6. Assign practitioners to observe a classroom situation for 15 minutes, recording in narrative format observations exemplifying low, moderate, or high teacher control models. Observations will be discussed on Day 2.

Day 2

1. Allow original teams formed during Day 1 10 minutes to analyze the findings of their observations.

2. As a whole group, discuss findings relative to the control environments observed. Record observations and examples on Classroom Management Chart.

Evaluation: Practitioners will have observed a classroom setting using a narrative format to document practices within the classroom indicative of low, moderate, or high teacher control styles; then, discuss findings with the whole group.

Debriefing:
1. Was there a control level that seemed to be predominant? Explain possible reasons for this.

2. In which control level do you feel most comfortable? Why?

3. Was there evidence that the level of control changed with the context of a situation? What might advantages and disadvantages be to this change?

4. Why is it important to record only observable behaviors?

5. At what point are practitioners' inferences justifiable?

6. How might data collected using a narrative format be used?

7. What are advantages and disadvantages to using a narrative format for documenting observations?

Table 3.4 Definition: Classroom Management

Actions and strategies practitioners use to encourage students to act within acceptable limits so that achievement may be attained.

Promoting Reflective Thinking in Teachers: 44 Action Strategies
by G. L. Taggart and A. P. Wilson. Copyright © Corwin Press, 1998.

Table 3.5 Synopsis of Classroom Management Styles

Low Teacher Control

The central philosophical beliefs behind the low teacher control approach are that students are primarily responsible for controlling their behavior and that they have the capacity for decision making. The practitioner's responsibility is to structure the learning environment to facilitate students' control and learning and to enforce an orderly environment. Student autonomy is evidenced by their assistance in the development of expectations.

Proponents of low control approaches are Berne, with his idea of transactional analysis, and Redl and Wattenberg's group management. Transactional analysis stems from questioning and analysis of verbal interactions. The approach was originated by Berne in his book, *Games People Play* (1964). Redl and Wattenberg's *Mental Hygiene in Teaching* (1959), later summarized by Redl in *When We Deal With Children* (1972), explains group management.

Berne contends that individuals possess three ego states—parent, child, and adult—which develop through life experiences and are either consciously or subconsciously held. The parent ego state pertains to parent and substitute parent influences that have helped us develop rules, norms, and mores. The child ego state develops from experiences in childhood, which tend to be more compulsive and expressive. The preferred adult ego state tends to provide rationality and problem-solving techniques for learners. Berne advocates that practitioners and students alike should strive to remain in this state to promote communication, positive relationships, and rational decision making.

Redl and Wattenberg advocate group management techniques to maintain control and to strengthen emotional development. Key features of the techniques are

Individuals act differently in groups than they do in individual settings.

Group dynamics vary within, between, and among groups.

Group behavior is determined by the perceptions of adult roles.

Diagnostic thinking can aid practitioners in determining underlying causes of behavior. Prior to practitioner interaction, determination of motivation, interaction dynamics, and future behaviors after intervention will foster positive responses.

continued

Table 3.5 Continued

Moderate Teacher Control

The central philosophical beliefs behind the moderate teacher control approach are (a) that practitioners and students are jointly responsible for controlling behavior and development and (b) that people are motivated by a need to belong and be accepted by others. The practitioner's responsibility is to structure the learning environment to facilitate students' control yet place the needs of the group as a whole ahead of individual students' needs. The practitioners also enforce rules and assist students in recognizing consequences of decisions and actions. Students are provided with opportunities to control their behavior and to jointly develop classroom rules and consequences with the practitioner.

Proponents of moderate control approaches are Dreikurs, who suggests logical consequences; Nelsen, who advocates *Positive Discipline* (1987); Glasser, who promotes reality therapy and control theory in *Schools Without Failure* (1969); and Kounin, who published *Discipline and Group Management in Classrooms* (1970). Dreikurs, using the work of Adler, supports the idea that acceptance is a large part of success in development. Logical consequences, events arranged by the teacher that are directly and logically related to a behavior, is used extensively in Dreikurs's democratic approach. He identifies three techniques leading to logical consequences. First, determine the goal for the behavior or misbehavior and confront the student with the goal for verification. Second, react to the misbehavior after rationally determining best alternatives for the action. Discussion of alternatives with the student is encouraged. Third, use encouragement statements to promote the use of positive alternatives.

Nelsen adapts Dreikurs's approach into a program called *positive discipline.* Kindness, respect, firmness, and encouragement are important to promoting positive behaviors. Key components are

Natural and logical consequences that foster positive classroom atmosphere

Understanding that there are four goals in behavior: attention, power, revenge, and respect

Expression of kindness and firmness when dealing with misbehavior

Mutual respect

Use of family and class meetings

Encouragement that fosters self-evaluation

SOURCE: Adapted from *Classroom Management and Discipline: Methods to Facilitate cooperation and Instruction* by Paul R. Burden. Copyright © 1995 by Longman Publishers USA. Reprinted by permission of Addison Wesley Educational Publishers, Inc. permission from Burden (1995).

continued

Table 3.5   Continued

Glasser's ideology of classroom management has changed since his first book, *Schools Without Failure,* appeared in 1969. Initially, reality therapy promoted the idea that students were responsible for choices and that they must live with the natural consequences of those choices. Practitioners and students jointly prepare rules and consequences. Practitioners are responsible for enforcing the rules and consequences by requiring students to make value judgments about misbehaviors. Practitioners are then responsible for suggesting possible consequences that are agreed on by both the practitioner and the student. Control theory added the need to belong, to love, and to control, and the needs for freedom and fun to the existing philosophy of reality therapy. In 1992, Glasser published *The Quality School.* The central philosophy that supports meeting the needs of students was expanded to advocate that school management must be reorganized to help meet student needs and promote effective learning. *The Quality School Teacher* (1993) is Glasser's latest book and provides strategies for meeting the needs of students in quality schools.

The Kounin model, based upon a philosophy expressed in *Discipline and Group Management in Classrooms* (1970), describes lessons and management strategies that can be used to prevent and to address misbehavior. Kounin uses the term *withitness* to describe the reaction of teachers to misbehaviors in a timely and appropriate fashion. When referring to simultaneous misbehaviors, Kounin refers to *overlapping.* To be an effective practitioner, withitness during overlapping events is required.

Movement management is another key area in Kounin's philosophy. Momentum, pacing, and transition are essential skills controlled by the practitioner for maintaining classroom control. Kounin suggests there are two mistakes related to movement management that cause practitioners difficulties. First, *jerkiness,* which refers to changes in the pacing of activities, which prompts misbehavior. Second, *slowdowns* are delays or wasted moments that occur because of overdwelling or fragmentation. Other misbehaviors may occur because of satiation with a topic or because of a ripple effect of misbehaviors.

High Teacher Control

The central philosophical belief behind the high teacher control approach is that students' growth and development are a result of external environmental conditions. The practitioner's responsibility is to select and reinforce desirable behaviors and extinguish undesirable behaviors. Few choices are given to students, as adults are more capable of providing direction and making choices.

SOURCE: Adapted from *Classroom Management and Discipline: Methods to Facilitate Cooperation and Instruction* by Paul R. Burden. Copyright © 1995 by Longman Publishers USA. Reprinted by permission of Addison Wesley Educational Publishers, Inc. permission from Burden (1995).

continued

Table 3.5   Continued

Proponents of high-control approaches are Skinner, Canter, and Dobson. Skinner is predominantly known for his philosophy of behavior modification first published in *Beyond Freedom and Dignity* (1971). Behavior modification deals with reinforcement or punishment techniques for shaping behavior. The responsibility of the practitioners lies in providing reinforcements, or rewards, when desired behaviors are accomplished and providing punishment for the performance of undesirable acts. Behavior modification is an organized, systematic model that must be applied consistently. Several techniques of behavior modification are

     Catch them being good.

     Ignore or praise rule breaking or keeping.

     Reward or punish rule keeping or breaking.

     Use contingency or "token" management systems.

     Contract for desired behavior.

Canter's (1976) goal for assertive discipline is to teach students to act responsibly and by doing so, to increase self-esteem and academic success. The practitioner's roles are

     To establish rules and directions clearly defining the limits of acceptable and unacceptable behavior

     Teach the rules and directions

     Request assistance from parents or administrators when needed

Canter's assertive discipline plan has three parts: rules, positive recognition that results from desirable behaviors, and consequences that result from misbehaviors.

Dobson (1970), in his book *Dare to Discipline,* maintains that healthy, happy children come from environments where there is a balance between love and control. Permissiveness is not allowed as children must be taught self-discipline and responsible behavior. Practitioners have the responsibility to establish boundaries and enforce consequences, giving children the "maximum reason to comply with your wishes" (p. 118). Dobson advocates infrequent use of corporal punishment in situations such as dangerous conditions, defiance, or temper tantrums. Preferred punishments are spanking, time-out, or loss of privileges.

SOURCE: Adapted from *Classroom Management and Discipline: Methods to Facilitate Cooperation and Instruction* by Paul R. Burden. Copyright © 1995 by Longman Publishers USA. Reprinted by permission of Addison Wesley Educational Publishers, Inc. permission from Burden (1995).

Table 3.6 Classroom Management Approaches

Level of Control	Level of Control	Proponents
Low Teacher Control	Transactional analysis	Eric Berne
	Congruent communication	Fritz Redl
	Group management	William Wattenberg
Moderate Teacher Control	Logical consequences	Rudolph Dreikurs
	Encouragement	Jane Nelsen
	Cooperative discipline	William Glasser
	Reality therapy	Jacob Kounin
	Control therapy	
	Lesson and group management	
High Teacher Control	Structured classrooms	B. F. Skinner
	Behavior modification	Lee Canter
	Assertive discipline	James Dobson
	Corporal punishment	

SOURCE: Adapted from *Classroom Management and Discipline: Methods to Facilitate Cooperation and Instruction* by Paul R. Burden. Copyright © 1995 by Longman Publishers USA. Reprinted by permission of Addison Wesley Educational Publishers, Inc. permission from Burden (1995).

Table 3.7   Classroom Management Chart

Type of Control	Indicators
Low	
Moderate	
High	

Dialectical Level

Practitioners reflecting at a dialectical level address problems with self-confidence and incorporate moral, ethical, and sociopolitical issues into decision making. They welcome peer review and question actions in a constant quest for workable alternatives. The following two lessons will assist practitioners in making observations dealing with a wide scope of alternatives, collaborating to improve instruction, and interpreting data collected from observations.

Task 13   Belief Systems: Their Role in Observational Learning

Topic: Observational learning

Objective: The practitioner will categorize observations made within a 15-minute period according to those activities necessary for instruction and those considered unnecessary based on current belief systems.

Materials: Observation Chart (Table 3.8); 3" × 5" index cards in three to five colors; one 5' newsprint section attached to the wall for each team; markers

Time: One 30-minute period; one 15-minute peer classroom observation period; one 50-minute period

Procedure: Day 1

1. Distribute a 3" × 5" colored note card to each practitioner. Practitioners will individually write five personal beliefs about educating students on their cards. Allow 5 minutes.

2. Group practitioners into teams of three to five according to the color of note card on which beliefs were written.

3. Allow team members to discuss commonalities and variances in beliefs. Encourage disclosure of past experiences prompting the beliefs. Allow 20 minutes.

4. Group practitioners back into a whole-group situation. Distribute and briefly discuss the Observation Chart. The task for practitioners is to observe in a mentor's or team member's classroom for 15 minutes using the Observation Chart. The completed chart will be discussed on Day 2.

Day 2

1. Practitioners will be grouped in the same teams formed on Day 1. Each team will elect a leader. Allow 10 minutes for teams to discuss the observation instrument and results of the observation.

2. Each team will prepare a list of beliefs deemed important for successful achievement in the classroom. Record those beliefs using markers onto the newsprint hung about the room. Three or four observational indicators should be listed under each belief that supports the belief statement. Allow 15 minutes.

continued

Task 13 Continued

3. Allow 15 minutes for teams to rotate clockwise about the room discussing listed beliefs and indicators. Look for commonalities and dissimilarities with the leader recording comments.

4. Call randomly on members of each team to briefly explain the team's discussions.

Evaluation: Practitioners categorized observations according to belief systems and participated actively in team discussion.

Debriefing: 1. What general statements can be made regarding the belief systems of practitioners in this session?

2. Were indicators for some beliefs more difficult to observe than others?

3. Which practitioners modified a belief statement based on observations? On team discussion?

4. Which practitioners modified actions based on their observations and belief statements?

5. Explain some of the universal beliefs regarding education.

Table 3.8 Observation Chart

Observation	N	U	Belief System

N = necessary; U = unnecessary

Task 14   Interpreting Change

Topic: Observational learning

Objective: The practitioner will (a) reflect on a classroom event that illustrates a change in philosophy, practice, or attitude; (b) analyze and clarify reasons for the change; and (c) determine attitude toward the change.

Materials: Note paper and pen; Dimensions of Change (either display copy or hand-outs—Table 3.9); clear transparencies

Time: 40 minutes

Procedure:
1. Ask practitioners to freely write for a 5-minute period regarding an event observed or experienced in a classroom situation that illustrates a change in philosophy, practice, or attitude on their part.

2. Pair practitioners by allowing each person to work with a partner with whom they are comfortable so as to create a risk-free environment.

3. Discuss the Dimensions of Change. Ask pairs of practitioners to view their writings in terms of these dimensions, taking notes on discussion elements. Allow 10 minutes.

4. Bring the whole group back together to discuss change. Endeavor to get practitioners to reflect on attitudes of change, possible reasons for change, and possible reasons not to change. Use a clear transparency on the overhead to list comments.

Evaluation: Practitioners will reflect on change individually, in pairs, and in whole-group discussion.

Debriefing:
1. Why is change so difficult?

2. How were you able to make the change? Was it lasting? Why or why not?

3. What helps practitioners bring about lasting, meaningful change?

4. Express your views on the dimensions of change.

5. Explain the value in time and effort regarding the effectiveness of changing to reflective thinking.

Table 3.9   Dimensions of Change

Change . . .

- Is multidimensional

- Varies within individuals as well as within groups

- Involves skills, practice, attitudes, and theory

- Relates to occupational identity, sense of competency, and self-concept

- Consists of dynamic interrelationships between and among other dimensions

- Must be defined relative to concrete individuals and situations

- Reasons must be sound

- Is difficult to achieve with any depth

- Must be of value to be meaningful

Reflective Questions

1. How can observational learning be better used in existing classroom situations?

2. Explain the place of observational learning in the field of administration.

3. What aspects of observational learning are the most beneficial to your continued growth in reflective thinking?

Action Assignments

Technical

1. Experience additional controlled observation sessions using taped vignettes.

2. Observe a child's exploration of new uses for old objects in a classroom situation (e.g., old socks for puppets, Styrofoam cups for gardens, etc.).

Contextual

1. Observe appropriate uses of cooperative learning strategies, using a narrative form of documentation. Discuss instrumentation that would make this observational learning process easier (e.g., a tally chart listing the key components of cooperative learning as the observational focus).

2. Observe student and practitioner experiences and reactions to the use of new manipulative devices (e.g., use of Cuisenaire rods in making fraction trains for determining equivalent fractions).

Dialectical

1. Experience additional controlled observations using taped vignettes that deal with ethical issues in teaching.

2. Consider the moral, ethical, and sociopolitical implications of classroom observation.

Suggestions for Success

1. Provide a risk-free environment.

2. Allow ample time for discussion of observations.

3. Some practitioners find that the observation instrument for assessing clear directions is too complex. It may be necessary to break the instrument into more manageable components, especially for preservice practitioners.

Journaling Reflective Growth

1. How can classroom observations increase reflective thinking?

2. Explain the aspects of observational learning that you would feel comfortable using in the classroom on an ongoing basis. What could be done to facilitate the aspects of observational learning that you feel uncomfortable using in the classroom?

3. Explain your growth in your ability to reflect.

Writing
Reflective Journals

4

I am struck continually by the isolation, the loneliness of teaching. The dialogue journal is one way to alter this isolation, and as such, it represents an essential human truth: we become and remain human not through the acquisition of factual knowledge or skills, but through participation in social communities.

—*Staton (1987, p. 60)*

Chapter Objectives

The facilitator will

Assist practitioners in demonstrating proficiency in the use of the journaling strategy

Be able to assess growth in reflective thinking on application of the strategy

Analyze personal competence of the strategy to assist practitioners in preparing action plans that will foster personal reflection on return to the classroom situation

Facilitate maintenance of reflective journals to be used by practitioners for personal growth assessment and for peer assessment

The Use of Reflective Journals

Posner (1996) states that more learning is derived from reflecting on an experience than is derived from the experience itself. Reflective journaling assists practitioners by making practice more educative, reveals Oberg (as cited in Clift, Houston, & Pugach, 1990). Educative practice provides consistency between practice and the beliefs and values of practitioners.

The type of journal used by this author for the purpose of enhancing reflective thinking is the dialogue journal. Copeland (as cited in Clift et al., 1990) cautions that journal writing contributes to reflection when practitioners are taught journaling techniques and receive thoughtful, meaningful feedback. The dialogue journal allows the reflective practitioner the opportunity to gain the benefits of journal writing. In addition, it provides facilitators with a tool for responding to events and to reflections on events by practitioners. Dialogue occurs when the facilitator responds to journal entries either through discussion or through written entries. Written entries may be made in the margins of the journal or on Post-it notes for placement in the journal. Care should be taken by the practitioner and facilitator to maintain subject anonymity and educational integrity. Responding to journaling may seem overwhelming. However, responding to a few journals a day or collecting journals periodically for responses will make the task manageable.

The dialogue journal is a widely used method of recording events and personal vignettes. The journal provides its author with an opportunity to chronicle over a period of time, then reflect on events. Dialogue journals may describe the episode, analyze cause and effect, and attempt to determine roles and beliefs stemming from the event. Assumptions and responses may be noted and analyzed as well as relationships between the event and traditionally held beliefs, traditions, or theories. For clarity of documentation, it is best that the dialogue journal entry be made as soon as possible following the event. Subsequent notes may be made at later dates once the initial entry has been made (Posner, 1996).

Norton (1994) contends that explicit guidelines; topics that compliment discussions and vice versa; and extensive, probing feedback from the mentor responding to the journal are instrumental in development of reflective thinking through journal writing. According to Posner (1996), a general format for dialogue journals would include

- Date and time of the entry
- Brief sequencing of the events of the day
- Elaboration on details of one or two episodes based on level of excitement, puzzlement, or confirmation

- Analysis of the episode
    - Possible explanations for event
    - Significance of the event
    - What was learned
    - Questions raised
    - Relevance
    - Responsibility on the part of the practitioner

Numerous benefits exist as a result of journal use in promoting reflective thinking (Bolin, 1988; Copeland, as cited in Clift et al., 1990; Garman, 1986; Houston & Clift, 1990; Yinger & Clark, 1981; Zeichner & Liston, 1987; Zinsser, 1988). Journals provide the reflective practitioner with means of

- Analyzing and reasoning through a dilemma
- Enhancing development and reflection
- Promoting growth in critical analysis of teaching
- Promoting awareness of relationships between educational psychology and practical experiences
- Systematically reflecting on self-development and on actions within classroom and work contexts
- Practicing reflective inquiry
- Building understanding by writing about what is learned
- Linking understanding with classroom practice

Journals provide the facilitator with a means for

- Challenging, supporting, and monitoring a practitioner's reflective thinking
- Promoting questions and discussion in educational course work and field experiences
- Analyzing teacher development, learning perspectives, and current level of understanding
- Guiding instruction
- Qualitatively analyzing instruction or a program
- Effectively maximizing staff development

The facilitator is to promote discussion of the use and value of dialogue journals as a learning and reflective tool. Activities are written at each of the three reflective levels: technical, contextual, and dialectical. Activities selected should be based on the experiences of the practitioners and levels of reflective thinking determined by the Profile of Reflective Thinking Attributes (Form 2.1). Level of reflection within journal entries may be determined by using the authors' Reflective Thinking Pyramid (Figure 1.1), Sparks-Langer et al.'s (1991) Framework for Reflective Thinking (Table 2.1), or Hattan and Smith's (1995) writing analysis guidelines described in Chapter 2.

Reflective Activities

Technical Level

At a technical level, practitioners have not had many experiences on which to formulate solutions to problematic classroom situations. The following activities will assist practitioners in organizing observations into a format that promotes reflective thinking, by raising levels of awareness and meaning of observations and by providing documentation from which information can be gathered for group discussion.

Task 15   Formatting a Journal Entry

Topic: Reflective journaling

Objective: The practitioner will analyze journal entries to develop a general format for preparing journal entries.

Materials: Transparency of Journal Entry (Table 4.1); individual copies of Journal Entry I and Journal Entry II (Tables 4.2 & 4.3); transparency of Benefits of Using Reflective Journals (Table 4.4); transparency and individual copies of Dialogue Journal Format (Table 4.5); clear transparencies

Time: 50 minutes

Procedure: 1. In a whole group, discuss with practitioners the benefits of journaling (Table 4.4). Inform practitioners that when first starting to use a journal, it is often best to follow a specific format until a comfort level is reached.

2. Read Journal Entry (Table 4.1) to practitioners as they view it on the overhead projector. On a clear transparency, list suggestions presented by practitioners from the journal entry that would make journaling easier. Possible suggestions are listed on the Dialogue Journal Format (Table 4.5).

3. When brainstorming on format items is complete (allow 5 minutes), place the Dialogue Journal Format on the overhead projector. Distribute copies and discuss format with practitioners.

4. Distribute copies of Journal Entry I and Journal Entry II. Ask practitioners to pair with a partner to review journal entries to determine if format was followed. A leader, the person with the longest hair, will report discussion results.

5. Use Dialogue Journal Format (Table 4.5) on the overhead projector to discuss with whole group the benefits of such a format and the value of the format to novice journal writers.

Evaluation: Practitioners became acquainted with journal format by analyzing journal entries.

Debriefing: 1. How might the journaling format be amended to fit time constraints?

2. By using a set format, do you feel reflection is helped or hindered? Explain your response.

3. Do you agree with the statement, "When people write about something, they learn it better"? Explain your response.

4. What type of response from your supervisor or peer would you most like to see written in your dialogue journal?

Promoting Reflective Thinking in Teachers: 44 Action Strategies
by G. L. Taggart and A. P. Wilson. Copyright © Corwin Press, 1998.

Table 4.1 Journal Entry

November 12   8:30 a.m.

Today the students had an Awards Assembly. Certain individuals were awarded for being good citizens, missing no school, etc. I think this is another neat thing this school does. It gives the students a sense of pride and helps build self-esteem. This reinforcement encourages positive behaviors that will stay with these individuals for a lifetime. Building self-esteem is so important at this age level as well as other developmental stages.

With the short amount of class time left, the teacher taught the students to count by five's. Since we were studying about Pilgrims, and there were 102 Pilgrims on the *Mayflower* when coming to America, we counted by five's up to 100, then added two to make 102.

Amber

Table 4.2 Journal Entry I

November 9   8:30–10:00 a.m.

Today, Ms. W. had a substitute teacher. It was a great experience for me because I saw from direct observation what a substitute teacher deals with as well as what Ms. W. comes back to. I guess this is when a teacher's flexibility comes in. We started the morning with Total Reading. The substitute knew a little background on it because her daughter goes to first grade in the same building. However, she did not approach it like Ms. W., which bothered the children. The children let her know she wasn't saying the chants fast enough. She also did not write phrases on the board correctly. (Ms. W. usually has a lined ruling and demonstrates exactly how it should look on the paper.) Finally, she hardly knew any hand signals, which some of the children depend on. I know it would be impossible for her to do things like Ms. W., but it really seemed to bother the children and affected their performance.

We also didn't get everything done that we were supposed to. I'm sure Ms. W. gave us plenty, though, so we wouldn't run out of things to do. A few directions were also vague, which made it difficult to know what she wanted. We basically followed the same routine, and the children were pretty good. They definitely let the substitute know when she wasn't doing something right. I think it would be very difficult to be a substitute teacher, because there is no way to prepare, and he or she walks in to the classroom blind. Also, Ms. W. will have to readjust to whatever didn't get done or wasn't done right. Even though it was a little frustrating and chaotic, I'm glad I had this experience. It was a real eye-opener!

Dean

Table 4.3   Journal Entry II

November 13   7:30–10:00 a.m.

Faculty Meeting
Journaling
Work on reports

   I began the day by attending a faculty meeting. Every Monday morning, faculty have a meeting from 7:30 a.m. till about 9:00 a.m. A parent
stays and supervises each home room during this time. I think this is a
good idea, for the faculty to meet and discuss issues every week. On
Monday, there is a different schedule due to this meeting.
   When the students arrived for class, I was surprised by the various
sizes of the students. There was quite a range for the same age and
grade level. I was also surprised by how the students behaved. They
were relatively quiet as they went about their business. When following
directions, the students again were quiet and got right to the point. If
any talking was going on, it was through a light whisper.
   Next, the class wrote on a given topic in their journals. The teacher
does not read what they write but makes sure that each entry is at least
seven lines. They have 5 minutes to complete their entry and are timed
with a timer. This process is done at the beginning of every class period.
While observing, I noticed a couple of boys not writing very much. I was
surprised by this. These are easy points to receive. All the teacher wants
from them is to count the number of lines. All it takes for the students
to receive the points is a small effort. Yet some of the students don't
care enough to make that effort. A boy from another class didn't even
write anything. He just drew a picture. Even after he realized that the
teacher and I knew what he was doing, he continued drawing. When it
was time to put the journals away, he proudly showed one of his friends
the drawing. It was clear to me that he did this for attention and to
impress his fellow students. I was amazed!

continued

Table 4.3   Continued

Every Monday morning, the teacher writes the weekly agenda on the board. The students are given time to copy it into their agenda notebooks. The school supplies each student with one of these notebooks. I think this is a super idea! What a great way to prepare students for high school and college. It is also a great way to promote responsibility and teach organizational skills. I was really impressed by this idea!

The students had short stories that were due. They had the opportunity to either 1) read their short story aloud themselves, 2) have the teacher read their stories without telling who wrote them, or 3) not have them read at all. The teacher had planned on the students responding, but only one student had his paper read. I was really impressed with his paper. It was 17 pages long (typed) and had a high vocabulary content. The teacher had to change her plans since no one wanted their stories read. She sent them to the library instead, which she originally had planned for tomorrow. Once again, teachers need to be flexible! I have to say I wasn't really surprised by the response the teacher received. The students are at an age where they would be embarrassed or self-conscious. They are too worried about what their peers might think.

One other thing I would like to comment on is that I think middle school lessons are easier to prepare. The teacher did the exact same thing every class period. She only had to prepare for one lesson, whereas an elementary teacher has to prepare for several. It is clear it takes more preparation for an elementary teacher than a middle school one.

Ann

Table 4.4   Benefits of Using Reflective Journals

- Analyzing and reasoning through a dilemma

- Enhancing development and reflection

- Promoting growth in critical analysis of teaching

- Promoting awareness of relationships between educational psychology and practical experiences

- Systematically reflecting on self-development and on actions within classroom and work contexts

- Practicing reflective inquiry

- Building understanding by writing about what is learned

- Linking understanding with classroom practice

Table 4.5 Dialogue Journal Format

- Date and time of the entry

- Brief sequencing of the events of the day

- Elaboration on details of one or two episodes based on level of excitement, puzzlement, or confirmation

- Analysis of the episode, possible explanations for event, significance of the event, what was learned, questions raised, relevance

SOURCE: Adapted from Posner (1996), *Field Experience: A Guide to Reflective Thinking.*
© Addison-Wesley, 1996; reprinted by permission of Addison-Wesley Educational Publishers, Inc.

Task 16 Journaling the Reflective Thinking Process

Topic: Reflective journaling

Objective: The practitioner will observe a classroom environment to document instances of the use of the Reflective Thinking Model.

Materials: Display copy of Reflective Thinking Model (Figure 1.2); individual copies of Dialogue Journal Format (Table 4.5); individual copies of Journal Entry II (Table 4.3)

Time: Two 30-minute periods; one 15-minute classroom observation period

Procedure: Day 1

NOTE: Norton (1994) states two requirements when using dialogue journaling as a catalyst for promoting and refining reflective thinking: (a) explicit format and (b) journal topics that are discussed or responded to on an ongoing basis. This is especially true when dealing with particular problems.

1.   Distribute Dialogue Journal Format.

2.   Review with practitioners the Reflective Thinking Model.

3.   Group practitioners in pairs by allowing them to partner with a colleague. The leader will be the practitioner with the longest time in current field setting.

4.   Distribute copies of Journal Entry II. Instruct practitioners to read the journal entry to ascertain the use of the Reflective Thinking Model by the individual observed. Allow 10 minutes.

5.   Discuss in a whole group the findings of each pair by calling on the leaders to report on the team's discussion.

6.   Assign practitioners a 15-minute classroom observation period with the intent of journaling instances using the Reflective Thinking Model. Journal entries will be discussed on Day 2.

                    continued

Task 16 Continued

Day 2

1. Allow 10 minutes for the pairs formed on Day 1 to caucus regarding their findings and journal entries.

2. Select two or three teams to role-play the Reflective Thinking process observed and journaled by one of the team members.

3. Use the Reflective Thinking Model to evaluate the process used.

Evaluation: Practitioners observed, journaled, and dialogued about use of the Reflective Thinking Model in the classroom.

Debriefing: 1. How difficult was it to observe the use of the Reflective Thinking Model?

2. Explain the usefulness of the Reflective Thinking Model in journaling episodes.

3. Explain the usefulness of role-playing and discussion in clarifying the Reflective Thinking Model.

4. How might observation and journaling make you a more effective practitioner? A more reflective practitioner?

Contextual Level

Practitioners reflecting at a contextual level are able to observe a class-room situation, analyze episodes based on context, assess appropriateness of actions relative to the needs of students, and relate actions to a theoretical base. The following two activities will assist practitioners in using journaling and feedback to analyze complex situations, comparing and contrasting episodes dealing with a like concept, and interpreting the relationship between practice and theory.

Task 17 A Comparison of the Use of Journaling to an Observational Checklist

Topic: Reflective journaling

Objective: The practitioner will observe a classroom situation to record an episode involving clarity in giving directions, using an observation instrument or journaling. Comparison of the actions recorded will be made through group discussions.

Materials: Individual copies (enough for half of the practitioners) of Observational Checklist of Behaviors Indicative of Giving Clear Directions (Table 4.6); individual copies (enough for half of the practitioners) of Dialogue Journal Format (Table 4.5); two journal entries volunteered by practitioners copied onto clear transparencies; clear transparencies

Time: Two 30-minute periods; one 15-minute classroom observation period

Procedure: Day 1

1. Distribute Dialogue Journal Format to half of the practitioners and the Observational Checklist of Behaviors Indicative of Giving Clear Directions to the other half. Instruct practitioners possessing the Dialogue Journal Format to pair up with someone holding the Observational Checklist. Explain that practitioners will be making observations regarding giving directions using one of the two techniques for recording.

2. Allow pairs of practitioners 5 minutes to compare the two techniques as to advantages and disadvantages of technique and decide on which person will be the recorder and which will be the reporter for the team.

3. Discuss in the whole group the comparisons derived from dyad discussions. List, using clear transparencies, advantages and disadvantages of each technique.

4. Instruct practitioners to use the observation instrument or journal for a 15-minute period in individual classroom assignments, observing the quality of directions presented to students.

continued

Task 17   Continued

Day 2

1. Allow 5 minutes for the pairs formed on Day 1 to caucus regarding their findings on the use and value of each of the techniques.

2. Call on the reporter in several of the pairs to summarize the findings of the team. Allow other pairs to report, if desired.

Evaluation: Reflective comparisons were made of using observational checklist and journaling of an episode involving clarity in giving directions.

Debriefing: 1. Which individuals are more likely to prefer the checklist technique over journaling? What would be reasons for this?

2. As a reflective practitioner, state your technique of preference. Defend your preference.

3. The theory behind effective questioning is supported by research. How does the theory relate to actual classroom practice?

4. How do you know when you are improving in reflective thinking ability?

Table 4.6 Observational Checklist of Behaviors Indicative of Giving Clear Directions

Directions: Place a tally mark in the right-hand column each time an observation of the indicator is made during the observation period.

Behavior Indicator Observed	Tally
Steps are provided in a logical sequence	_____
1. Presented visually	_____
2. Presented verbally	_____
Steps are explained in detail	_____
1. Full explanation given	_____
2. Further explanation given, if necessary	_____
3. Steps repeated, if necessary	_____
Vocabulary appropriate for developmental level	_____
Steps are presented in a clear tone	_____
Steps are presented at an appropriate volume	_____
Steps are modeled for the students	_____
1. Each step in process shown visually	_____
2. Each step in process restated	_____
Students are encouraged to ask questions	_____
1. Through a verbal request	_____
2. Through teacher body language	_____
Students are asked questions to check for understanding	_____
1. Students called upon randomly	_____
2. Students called upon equitably	_____
3. Students asked clarifying questions, if needed	_____

Task 18   A Comparison of Observations With the Use of a Journaling Format to Observations Without the Use of a Journaling Format

Topic: Reflective journaling

Objective: The practitioner will observe a classroom situation to record an episode involving clarity in giving directions, journaling with or without a set format. Comparison of the actions recorded will be made through group discussions.

Materials: Individual copies (enough for half the practitioners) of Dialogue Journal Format (Table 4.5); two journal entries volunteered by practitioners, one from each team, copied onto clear transparencies; clear transparencies

Time: Two 30-minute periods; one 15-minute classroom observation period

Procedure: Day 1

1. Distribute Dialogue Journal Format to only half of the practitioners. Practitioners are not to share the format at this time. Explain that practitioners will be making observations regarding giving direction. Half will be using the format, the other half will be free to use a format of their choice while making classroom observations.

2. Allow practitioners possessing the format to team and those possessing no format to team. Allow 15 minutes for teams to discuss how they would go about journaling observations made.

3. Assign practitioners to journal for a 15-minute period in individual classroom assignments observing the quality of directions presented to children.

Day 2

1. Allow 15 minutes for the teams assigned on Day 1 to caucus regarding their findings on the journaling activity. Discuss advantages and disadvantages to using a format while journaling. Teams should also select a leader: the individual who has the longest journal entry.

2. Call on the leader to summarize the findings of the team. Clear transparencies may be used to categorize advantages and disadvantages.

Promoting Reflective Thinking in Teachers: 44 Action Strategies
by G. L. Taggart and A. P. Wilson. Copyright © Corwin Press, 1998.   *continued*

Task 18 Continued

Evaluation: Reflective comparisons of observations of an episode involving clarity in giving directions were made, with and without journaling format.

Debriefing: 1. Which individuals are more likely to prefer using a prescribed format? What would be reasons for this?

2. As a reflective practitioner, state your technique of preference. Defend your preference.

3. The theory behind effective questioning is supported by research. How does the theory relate to actual classroom practice?

4. How do you know when you are improving in reflective thinking ability?

Promoting Reflective Thinking in Teachers: 44 Action Strategies
by G. L. Taggart and A. P. Wilson. Copyright © Corwin Press, 1998.

Dialectical Level

Practitioners reflecting at a dialectical level address problems with self-confidence and incorporate moral, ethical, and sociopolitical issues into decision making. Peer review is welcomed as actions are constantly reviewed and updated as alternatives are sought. For these reasons, the following two lessons are open-ended. Practitioners will be assisted in making choices reflecting a wide variety of issues and alternatives.

Task 19   Open-Ended Journaling

Topic: Reflective journaling

Objective: The practitioner will devise a system of journaling that meets instructional needs and addresses issues on a dialectical level.

Materials: Prepared individual copies of Benefits of Using Reflective Journals (Table 4.4); clear transparencies

Time: Two 30-minute periods; three 15-minute classroom observation periods

Procedure: *Day 1*

1. Prepare Benefits of Journaling sheets by systematically writing at the bottom of each sheet one of these terms: *change, instructional innovation, professionalism, collegiality,* or *decision making.*

2. Discuss with whole group the benefits of journaling and distribute Benefits of Using Reflective Journals sheets.

3. Group practitioners into teams of three or four according to the terms written previously at the bottom of the handout. Teams are to devise a journaling format to be used in observing and addressing an issue under the general term for each team. For example, the team with the term "change" may devise a plan to observe and journal episodes involving such models as constructivism or team teaching. Allow 20 minutes.

4. In whole-group discussion, summarize the efforts of the teams. Discuss problem areas, challenges, and anticipations.

5. Assign practitioners to observe in a mentor or team member's classroom or school for three 15-minute periods and record observations that center around the issue using the journaling format devised.

Day 2

1. Practitioners will be grouped in the same teams formed in Day 1. Each team will elect a leader. Allow 15 minutes for teams to discuss topics, findings, and journaling processes.

2. Each team will use a clear transparency to illustrate its journaling format and the findings of its observations. The team leader will report findings to the whole group using the transparencies.

Promoting Reflective Thinking in Teachers: 44 Action Strategies
by G. L. Taggart and A. P. Wilson. Copyright © Corwin Press, 1998.

continued

Task 19 Continued

Evaluation: Practitioners prepared and used a journaling format to meet the needs of the topic assigned.

Debriefing: 1. What differences were noted in the various journaling formats presented? Similarities?

2. Explain the necessity of being flexible in using a journal format.

3. What made the topics presented challenging (or unchallenging) to observe and journal?

4. What other topic(s) would be of interest to you?

5. How can journaling efforts lead into action research?

Task 20   Rights and Responsibilities

Topic: Reflective journaling

Objective: The practitioner will journal events of an educational gathering reflecting on the rights and responsibilities of practitioners.

Materials: Five 3-ft newsprint sheets hung about the room, each labeled with one of the following terms: *community, parent empowerment, ethical issues, legal issues,* and *lifelong learning;* markers; clear transparencies

Time: One 45-minute period, one 15-minute observation period, and one 30-minute period

Procedure: Day 1

1. Group practitioners by having them move to one of the five newsprint sheets that most reflects a personal concern. Provide each group with a marker. Designate the practitioner with the lightest hair color as the reporter, the one with the darkest hair color as the recorder.

2. Groups are to discuss the term designated on the newsprint to determine one or two specific issues within that topic they would like to address.

3. Each group is to format a plan for each team member to observe and journal one episode related to one or both specific issues. The episode must be taken from an event outside regular classroom situations. For example, study groups, school board meetings, parent-teacher association meetings, university courses, and so on.

4. The recorder will write the format on the newsprint.

5. Bring the practitioners together into a whole-group situation. Each reporter will advise the group of the team plan.

6. Discuss challenges and concerns.

7. Assign each practitioner to observe in an educational setting for one 15-minute period and record observations that center around the issue chosen by the team using the format devised.

Promoting Reflective Thinking in Teachers: 44 Action Strategies
by G. L. Taggart and A. P. Wilson. Copyright © Corwin Press, 1998.   *continued*

Task 20   Continued

Day 2

1. Practitioners will be grouped in the same teams formed in Day 1. Allow 15 minutes for teams to discuss topics, findings, and journaling processes.

2. Each team will use a clear transparency to illustrate the journaling format and the findings of their observations. The team leader will report findings to the whole group using clear transparencies.

Evaluation: Practitioners prepared and used a journaling format to make observations on the topic assigned.

Debriefing: 1. What differences were noted in the various journaling formats presented? Similarities?

2. Is it necessary to be flexible in using a journaling format? Explain your rationale.

3. Were the topics presented challenging to observe and journal? If so, what made them so?

4. What other topic(s) would be of interest to you?

5. How can journaling efforts lead to action research?

Promoting Reflective Thinking in Teachers: 44 Action Strategies
by G. L. Taggart and A. P. Wilson. Copyright © Corwin Press, 1998.

Reflective Questions

1. How will journaling on a daily basis affect your teaching ability?
2. Identify a specific journal format that fit your personal needs better than others.
3. How do you feel about someone else reading and responding to your journal?
4. What actions may be taken with information journaled?
5. What ethical and legal reasons support the anonymity of locations and individuals discussed in journal entries?

Action Assignments

Technical

1. Provide additional controlled observations and journaling practice using taped vignettes.
2. Collect journal entries from willing practitioners, remove the names, make copies for review by other practitioners. Analyze the entries for format and level of reflection.

Contextual

1. Have participants observe one or two children having behavior problems in the classroom. Use journal entries over a period of time, coupled with possible interventions, to help determine the value of the interventions in extinguishing the unwanted behaviors.
2. Have participants obtain permission to walk into a classroom in which they have never been. During the first 5 minutes of arrival, they are to journal all they can regarding the physical environment of the room. Ask them to analyze their entry: Why were the items mentioned noticed in that short time period? How is this relevant to your own classroom situation?

Dialectical

1. Provide for additional observations of individuals: principals, superintendents, school psychologist, and so on. Determine the role of these individuals in the school community. Do the roles determined differ from preconceived notions? Why is that so?

2. Journal a negotiations meeting held by a local school district. Write only observable information. When the meeting is completed, add inferences gleaned from the observations. Is your perspective on the events of the meeting the same on reflection as during the time of your journaling?

Suggestions for Success

1. Start small. Use a format and controlled situations. Graduate to less formalism and more complex situations.

2. Practitioners should periodically review journal entries determining growth in knowledge, skills, and reflective thinking ability.

Journaling Reflective Growth

1. Will my use of journaling differ in the future because of increased knowledge about journaling?

2. Journaling is considered to be a form of reflection-on-action (Schön, 1987). An ultimate goal for reflective thinking is reflection-in-action. Do you feel that journaling will lead to reflection-in-action on your part? Why do you feel as you do?

3. Through journaling efforts thus far, are there topics that have sparked an interest for continued research? What might those topics be? Will they lend themselves to action research?

5
Using Practicum Strategies

Reflection becomes the essential link between lessons and proves to be the difference between teaching to meet district objectives and teaching to help all students understand.

—M. L. Schroeder (1996, p. 648)

Chapter Objectives

The facilitator will

Assist practitioners in demonstrating proficiency in the use of the practicum strategy

Be able to assess growth in reflective thinking upon application of the strategy

Analyze personal competence of the strategy to assist practitioners in preparing an action plan that will foster personal reflection upon return to the classroom situation

Facilitate maintenance of reflective journals to be used by practitioners for personal growth assessment and for peer assessment

Two practicum strategies will be discussed in this section: *micro-teaching* and *reflective teaching,* popularized by Cruickshank (1985). Both strategies provide practitioners with opportunities to plan and implement lessons, present the lessons to small cohort groups, then reflect on the outcome of the presentations. Lessons are usually brief, 5 to 15 minutes long, and cover a single teaching concept. The experience is low risk. The benefits, however, are high when the practicum experience is followed by thoughtful facilitator, peer, and self reflection.

The Microteaching Process

Microteaching has been a part of teacher preparation for the past three decades. As the name implies, microteaching is a simulated teaching experience of short duration, with the practitioner teaching a lesson to a small cohort group or to a small class of students. Orlich, Harder, Callahan, Kauchak, and Gibson (1994) provide the following rationale for the microteaching experience. Microteaching allows the practitioner to

- Practice a technique, strategy, or procedure
- Reduce anxiety by practicing in a supportive environment
- Test innovative approaches to a teaching concept
- Develop specific delivery strategies, such as questioning or closure
- Experience facilitator, peer, and self evaluation
- Gain immediate feedback of experiences
- Practice team teaching in a supportive environment

The procedure for teaching a microteaching lesson is simple. The practitioner first decides on the topic or process to teach and prepares a plan of the lesson. The format of the lesson is preestablished. Specific performance objectives are outlined on the plan as well as materials needed, time constraints, and procedures for teaching the lesson. A conclusion and evaluation of the lesson's effectiveness in producing the desired objective ends the lesson. The practitioner rehearses the lesson; prepares two copies of the plan, one to refer to while teaching, the other for the facilitator or peer; then teaches the lesson during a preset time period.

During the teaching experience, three formative evaluations are taking place. The first is the assessment by the facilitator of the microteaching. Using the copy of the plan, make written comments on the effectiveness of the plan to cover the objective, its portability, and the implementation of the plan by the practitioner. Be positive regarding strategies and concepts effectively used. Note improvements needed in a constructive manner.

The second formative evaluation is being conducted simultaneously. One or more peers of the practitioner are also rating the microteaching. They, however, do not have access to the lesson plan. Both the facilitator and peer reviewers should rate the practitioner using the rubric (see Task 23) prepared by the group prior to the microteaching experience.

Rubrics are used as an assessment tool. The rubric created by the practitioners provides a format for review of the teaching process. It allows for the practitioner to think about the important elements of the teaching episode and to reflect on teaching efficiencies and deficits. Ownership in the rubric is inherent in the fact that all practitioners participate in its construction (Taggart, Phifer, Nixon, & Wood, 1998).

During the course of the microteaching, the lesson is being videotaped by a peer or technician. The goal of videotaping is to capture the interaction of the classroom. Once the initial novelty wears off, both students and teacher accept the presence of the equipment and the technician, and the class proceeds with minimal disruptions. The videotaped lesson is reviewed first by the practitioners, who use the rubric for microteaching to critique their own lesson. The critiquing session may be handled privately by the practitioner as the third formative assessment. This review should be accomplished soon after the microteaching event. The tape and critique are reviewed at a later date simultaneously by the facilitator and practitioner. The practitioner explains his critique using the rubric, the video is viewed with comments made by either the practitioner or the facilitator, and the lesson plan with facilitator comments and peer critiques is given to the practitioner. It is at this time a final grade determination is made, if needed, and that goals are established for the next microteaching.

Reflective Teaching

An alternative peer teaching experience to microteaching is reflective teaching, developed by Cruickshank, Kennedy, Williams, Holton, and Fay (1981) at Ohio State University. Reflective teaching is a strategy for promoting thinking about the process of teaching. It was developed as a peer teaching technique with the intent of making teachers more thoughtful practitioners (Cruickshank et al., 1981).

Cruickshank et al.'s Reflective Teaching is intended to promote method and efficiency. The method has won the support of professional organizations, such as Phi Delta Kappa and the American Association of Colleges for Teacher Education, because of its use as a viable experiential teaching alternative. The major aims of the reflective teaching approach (Cruickshank, 1985; Cruickshank et al., 1981; see Table 5.1) are

- To provide a controlled clinical atmosphere with which to practice instructional skills
- To provide an opportunity to consider a teaching episode thoughtfully, analytically, and objectively
- To develop habits of reflective thought about teaching
- To provide for peer teaching
- To provide the designated teacher with immediate feedback and reflection opportunities
- To provide an easily transportable alternative teaching model requiring few materials and limited time and space

Table 5.1 Aims of Reflective Teaching

- To provide a controlled clinical atmosphere

- To provide an opportunity to consider a teaching episode thoughtfully, analytically, and objectively

- To develop habits of reflective thought about teaching

- To provide for peer teaching

- To provide immediate feedback and reflection opportunities

- To provide an alternative teaching model

SOURCE: Adapted with permission from Cruickshank (1985).

Criteria for using the reflective teaching strategy are few (Cruickshank, 1985). The lesson must be of high interest to the practitioner. Reflective teaching lessons focus on one of three domains: cognitive, psychomotor, or affective. Lessons are brief, taking no more than 15 minutes, are self-contained, and use a minimum of materials. Objectives for the lessons must be measurable.

There are numerous benefits to reflective teaching (see Table 5.2). Reflective teaching

- Provides a nonthreatening environment in which to practice
- Allows experimentation and sharing of teaching experiences
- Provides an atmosphere that promotes peer communication
- Fosters self-review and peer review of teaching skills
- Provides an opportunity to observe others
- Allows practitioners to come to value practical knowledge
- Improves articulation of knowledge
- Develops collegiality
- Makes for efficient use of time and money in providing teaching practice
- Provides practitioners with immediate feedback on teaching performance
- Focuses or refocuses on insights into teaching

Table 5.2   Reflective Teaching Benefits

- Provides a nonthreatening environment
- Allows experimentation and sharing of teaching experiences
- Promotes peer communication
- Fosters self-review and peer review of teaching
- Allows opportunity to observe others
- Allows practitioners to come to value practical knowledge
- Improves articulation of knowledge
- Develops collegiality
- Makes for efficient use of time and money in providing teaching practice
- Provides practitioners with immediate feedback on teaching performance
- Focuses on insights into teaching

SOURCE: Adapted with permission from Cruickshank (1985).

Reflective Activities

Technical

At a technical level, practitioners will be using Cruickshank's (1985) reflective teaching format to prepare and teach a lesson. Task 21, "The Anxiety Task," provides a teaching experience using the affective domain. Task 22, the "Lines of Symmetry Task," is a reflective teaching experience using the cognitive domain. Both activities support the need for practitioners reflecting at a technical level to make references to past experiences; to practice meeting a specified objective in a risk-free environment; and to focus on particular behavior, content, or skills.

Task 21   The Anxiety Task

Topic: Practicum strategies: Reflective teaching—Affective domain (Adapted from Cruickshank, 1987)

Objective: The practitioner will teach a reflective teaching lesson, then engage in a peer review of the lesson.

Materials: Sufficient copies of The Anxiety Task (Table 5.3) for groups of four to six practitioners; overhead transparencies of Aims of Reflective Teaching (Table 5.1) and Reflective Teaching Benefits (Table 5.2)

Time: One 10-minute period; one 40-minute period

Procedure: *Day 1*

1. Divide practitioners into groups of four to six, with the tallest individual being designated as the teacher. All team members will teach a lesson using the model as time permits. (Other lessons at the affective, cognitive, and psychomotor levels may be found in Cruickshank's [1987] *Reflective Teaching: The Preparation of Students of Teaching.*)

2. Provide the practitioners with a brief background and the aims and benefits of reflective teaching by using overhead transparencies for each topic.

3. Distribute to the designated teachers The Anxiety Task, instructing them that they will be expected to review the lesson and then teach the lesson to the remaining team members on Day 2. Each lesson consists of objectives, subject matter, materials, time limitations, and suggested guidelines. Concentration will be on the teaching process.

Day 2

1. Allow teaching time of no more than 15 minutes, which includes administration of the pretest and posttest.

2. At the end of the designated time period, instruct the designated teacher to give the Learner Satisfaction Forms to other team members and to compare the pretest and posttest evaluations. Allow 5 minutes.

3. The designated teacher will use the small group reflection form to lead discussion among the team members on the process of the teaching episode. Recording reflections made should be done during this time period. All materials should be collected by the facilitator for review. Allow 10 minutes.

continued

Task 21   Continued

4. During the remaining 10 minutes, the facilitator should lead the whole group in discussion of the debriefing questions.

5. On subsequent days, repeat the process so that all team members have a chance to become designated teachers.

Evaluation: Was the reflective teaching episode accomplished? Did the team members provide feedback to the designated teacher in a discussion format?

Debriefing: 1. In what various ways did the designated practitioners teach the reflective teaching lesson?

2. How successful was the methodology in bringing about learner satisfaction and achievement?

3. What happened to facilitate learning and satisfaction?

4. What, if anything, could be changed to increase learner achievement and satisfaction?

5. What was learned (rediscovered) about teaching or learning that may be worth reflecting on for later use?

6. To what extent was the designated teacher satisfied or dissatisfied with the teaching or learning, and why?

Table 5.3   Reflective Teaching Task: Affective Domain

Designated Teacher _____

Group Members   _____

_____

_____

_____

_____

The Anxiety Task

Description of Your Reflective Thinking Task

You are to teach this short lesson to a small group of your peers. The exercise is intended to provide an opportunity to experience teaching and then to reflect on the shared teaching-learning experience. Plan to teach it in such a way that you believe both learning and satisfaction will result.

Your lesson will be taught on _____ (date).

Introduction to the Lesson

Teachers foster attitude change—that is, they attempt to get students to change their minds about people, events, content to be learned, and so forth. The following are examples of teachers fostering attitude change:

1. A social studies teacher engages the class in a discussion of the contributions of persons of a variety of national origins to present-day American culture.

2. A foreign language teacher shows the class how learning a foreign language will be helpful in their everyday life.

3. A home economics teacher encourages boys to consider performing home tasks associated with assuming family responsibility.

Following is a goal that requires you to foster attitude change with a small group of your peers. The task was selected because your success in accomplishing it probably will not be dependent on your knowledge of some academic subject or previous experience you might have had.

SOURCE: Adapted with permission from Cruickshank (1985).   *continued*

Table 5.3 Continued

Your Goal

Your goal is to get as many of your learners as possible to change their attitudes toward the notion of anxiety. Specifically, you should try to get your learners to disagree with the following statements:

Anxiety breeds anxiety.

Anxiety increases performance.

Anxiety stems from lack of preparation.

Anxiety is a learned attitude.

You will have no more than 15 minutes in which to accomplish your goal.

Materials

1. Pretest
2. Posttest
3. Scoring sheet
4. Learner satisfaction forms
5. Group follow-up discussion questions

Special Conditions and Limitations

Before you begin teaching, obtain a copy of the pretest for each learner. Distribute the pretests and have learners respond to it. Collect the pretests before you start.

Ending the Lesson

Distribute copies of the posttest and the Learner Satisfaction Form. Give your learners the posttest, and when they are finished (no more than 2 minutes), return their pretests and ask them to indicate any changes that they may have made from pretest to posttest. Next, distribute the Learner Satisfaction Forms. While they are being completed, collect the pretests and posttests and record the scores in the scoring box on the Scoring Sheet. Return the pretests and posttests and collect the Learner Satisfaction Forms.

Begin to work through the questions for small-group discussion with your learners. Record responses from your group on the form provided. Put designated teacher's name and all group members' names on the top of page 1. Hand all materials to the instructor.

SOURCE: Adapted with permission from Cruickshank (1985).   *continued*

Table 5.3 Continued

Pretest for the Anxiety Task

Name _____

Following are statements about anxiety. Rate each on the basis of whether you agree or disagree with it by placing a check mark in one column after each statement. The check mark must be in a box and not on a line.

Statements	Strongly Agree	Agree	Disagree	Strongly Disagree
1. Anxiety breeds anxiety.				
2. Anxiety increases performance.				
3. Anxiety stems from lack of preparation.				
4. Anxiety is a learned attitude.				

SOURCE: Adapted with permission from Cruickshank (1985).

continued

Table 5.3   Continued

Posttest for the Anxiety Task

Name _____

Part A

Following are statements about anxiety. Rate each on the basis of whether you agree or disagree with it by placing a check mark in one column after each statement. The check mark must be in a box and not on a line.

Statements	Strongly Agree	Agree	Disagree	Strongly Disagree
1. Anxiety breeds anxiety.				
2. Anxiety increases performance.				
3. Anxiety stems from lack of preparation.				
4. Anxiety is a learned attitude.				

Part B

Do you think that your attitude toward anxiety has been modified somewhat by this Reflective Teaching experience? (Check one box)

_____ Yes

_____ No

SOURCE: Adapted with permission from Cruickshank (1985).   *continued*

Table 5.3 Continued

Scoring Sheet for the Anxiety Task

Once your learners have completed both the pretest and the posttest, you can count how many of them changed or did not change attitudes toward each statement in the desired direction.

NOTE: Each row (across) in the scoring box will total your number of learners.

Statements	*Number of Learners Who Changed Their Attitudes in the Desired Direction*	*Number of Learners Who Did Not Change Their Attitudes in the Desired Direction*
1. Anxiety breeds anxiety.		
2. Anxiety increases performance.		
3. Anxiety stems from lack of preparation.		
4. Anxiety is a learned attitude.		
Total (add down)		

From Part B on the Posttest

How many of your learners felt their attitudes were moderated toward anxiety from this experience? _____

SOURCE: Adapted with permission from Cruickshank (1985).

continued

Table 5.3   Continued

**Small-Group Discussion Questions
for the Reflective Teaching Task**

1. What probably most influenced the way this lesson was taught: the content, the learners, the context or setting, the teacher's views of and experiences with teaching, available materials, other? How did these factors probably affect how the lesson was taught?

2. Given the posttest results, to what extent did learners learn?

3. Based on the comments made on the Learner Satisfaction Forms, to what extent did instruction result in satisfaction?

4. What does the group believe contributed most to achievement and satisfaction?

5. What does the group believe got in the way of achievement and satisfaction?

6. What did you learn or recall about effective teaching and learning? Enumerate at least two insights.

7. How do you feel about the teaching-learning experience?

SOURCE: Adapted with permission from Cruickshank (1985).

continued

Table 5.3   Continued

Learner Satisfaction Form for the Reflective Teaching Lesson

Name _____

1. During the lesson, how satisfied were you as a learner?

    _____ Very satisfied

    _____ Satisfied

    _____ Unsatisfied

    _____ Very unsatisfied

2. Suggest anything and everything that could have been done to increase your satisfaction with the topic, the teaching, or achievement. Be as analytical and critical (in the best sense) as you possibly can. Your responsibility is to make the teacher think deeply about teaching and learning.

— —

Learner Satisfaction Form for the Reflective Teaching Lesson

Name _____

1. During the lesson, how satisfied were you as a learner?

    _____ Very satisfied

    _____ Satisfied

    _____ Unsatisfied

    _____ Very unsatisfied

2. Suggest anything and everything that could have been done to increase your satisfaction with the topic, the teaching, or achievement. Be as analytical and critical (in the best sense) as you possibly can. Your responsibility is to make the teacher think deeply about teaching and learning.

SOURCE: Adapted with permission from Cruickshank (1985).

Task 22   Lines of Symmetry Task

Topic: Practicum strategies: Reflective teaching—Affective domain (Adapted from Cruickshank, 1987)

Objective: The practitioner will teach a reflective teaching lesson, then engage in a peer review of the lesson.

Materials: Copies of Lines of Symmetry Task (Table 5.4) for groups of four to six practitioners; clear transparencies of Aims of Reflective Teaching (Table 5.1) and Reflective Teaching Benefits (Table 5.2).

Time: One 10-minute period; one 40-minute period

Procedure: *Day 1*

1. Divide practitioners into groups of four to six, with the tallest individual being designated as the teacher. All team members will teach a lesson using the model as time permits. (Other lessons at the affective, cognitive, and psychomotor levels may be found in Cruickshank's [1987] *Reflective Teaching: The Preparation of Students of Teaching.*)

2. Provide the practitioners with a brief background and the aims and benefits of reflective teaching by using the overhead transparencies for each topic.

3. Distribute to the designated teachers the Lines of Symmetry Task, instructing them that they will be expected to review the lesson and then teach the lesson to the remaining team members on Day 2. Each lesson consists of objectives, subject matter, materials, time limitations, and suggested guidelines. Concentration will be on the teaching process.

Day 2

1. Allow teaching time of no more than 15 minutes, which includes administration of the pretest and posttest.

2. At the end of the designated time period, instruct the designated teacher to give the Learner Satisfaction Forms to other team members and to compare the pretest and posttest evaluations. Allow 5 minutes.

continued

Task 22   Continued

3. The designated teacher will use the small-group reflection form to lead discussion among the team members on the process of the teaching episode. Recording reflections made should be done during this time period. All materials should be collected by the facilitator for review. Allow 10 minutes.

4. During the remaining 10 minutes, the facilitator should lead the whole group in discussion of the debriefing questions.

5. On subsequent days, repeat the process so that all team members have a chance to become designated teachers.

Evaluation: Was the reflective teaching episode accomplished? Did the team members provide feedback to the designated teacher in a discussion format?

Debriefing: 1. In what various ways did the designated practitioners teach the reflective teaching lesson?

       2. How successful was the methodology in bringing about learner satisfaction and achievement?

       3. What happened to facilitate learning and satisfaction?

       4. What, if anything, could be changed to increase learner achievement and satisfaction?

       5. What was learned (rediscovered) about teaching or learning that may be worth reflecting on for later use?

       6. To what extent was the designated teacher satisfied or dissatisfied with the teaching or learning, and why?

Table 5.4   Reflective Teaching Task: Cognitive Domain

Designated Teacher _____

Group Members   _____

_____

_____

_____

Lines of Symmetry Task

Description of Your Reflective Thinking Task

You are to teach this short lesson to a small group of your peers. The exercise is intended to provide an opportunity to experience teaching and then to reflect on the shared teaching-learning experience. Plan to teach it in such a way that you believe both learning and satisfaction will result.

Your lesson will be taught on _____ (date).

Introduction to the Lesson

Teachers foster cognitive change—that is, they attempt to get students to add concepts to their existing schema. The following are examples of teachers fostering cognitive change:

1. An elementary teacher describes how to perform addition and demonstrates by example.
2. A dance teacher describes how to do a step and demonstrates by example.
3. A chemistry teacher describes how to light a burner and demonstrates by example.
4. A physical education teacher describes how to do a flip and demonstrates by example.

Following is a goal that requires you to foster cognitive change with a small group of your peers. The task was selected because your success in accomplishing it probably will not be dependent on your knowledge of some academic subject or previous experience you might have had.

SOURCE: Adapted with permission from Cruickshank (1985).   *continued*

Table 5.4 Continued

Your Goal

Your goal is to get as many of your learners as possible to be able to correctly identify the lines of symmetry of a square, triangle, and the letters in their names. You will have 15 minutes in which to accomplish your objective.

Symmetry involves the use of a line or lines that promote(s) balance or a point about which a figure or design is rotated. It requires equity of parts. A line of symmetry may be drawn vertically across the center of a capital A. In contrast, a circle has an infinite number of lines of symmetry.

Materials

1. Pretest
2. Posttest
3. Scoring sheet
4. Learner satisfaction forms
5. Small-group follow-up discussion questions

Special Conditions and Limitations

Before you begin teaching, obtain a copy of the pretest for each learner. Distribute the pretests and have learners respond to it. Collect the pretests before you start.

Ending the Lesson

Distribute copies of the posttest and the Learner Satisfaction Form. Give your learners the posttest, and when they are finished (no more than 2 minutes), return their pretests and ask them to indicate any changes that they may have made from pretest to posttest. Next, distribute the Learner Satisfaction Forms, and while they are being completed, collect the pretests and posttests and record the scores in the scoring box on the Scoring Sheet. Return the pre- and posttests and collect the Learner Satisfaction Forms.

Begin to work through the questions for small-group discussion with your learners. Record responses from your group on the form provided. Put designated teacher's name and all group members' names on the top of page 1. Hand all materials to the instructor.

SOURCE: Adapted with permission from Cruickshank (1985).

continued

Table 5.4   Continued

Pretest for the Lines of Symmetry Task

Name _____

Identify the lines of symmetry for the following figures:

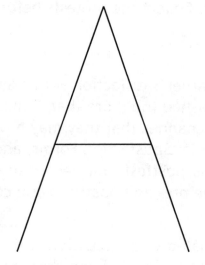

SOURCE: Adapted with permission from Cruickshank (1985).

continued

Table 5.4 Continued

Posttest for the Lines of Symmetry Task

Name _____

Identify the lines of symmetry for the following figures:

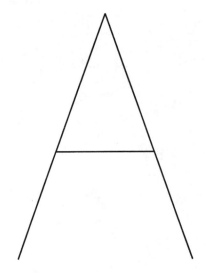

SOURCE: Adapted with permission from Cruickshank (1985).

continued

Table 5.4 Continued

Scoring Sheet for the
Lines of Symmetry Task

Once your learners have completed both the pretest and the posttest, you can count how many of them were able to learn the placement of the lines of symmetry in the square, triangle, and the letters of their names. Tally the correct responses for each test.

	Pretest	Posttest
Square		
Triangle		
Letters		

SOURCE: Adapted with permission from Cruickshank (1985).

continued

Table 5.4 Continued

Small-Group Discussion Questions for the Reflective Teaching Lesson

1. What probably most influenced the way this lesson was taught: the content, the learners, the context or setting, the teacher's views of and experiences with teaching, available materials, other? How did these factors probably affect how the lesson was taught?

2. Given the posttest results, to what extent did learners learn?

3. Based on the comments made on the Learner Satisfaction Forms, to what extent did instruction result in satisfaction?

4. What does the group believe contributed most to achievement and satisfaction?

5. What does the group believe got in the way of achievement and satisfaction?

6. What did you learn or recall about effective teaching and learning? Enumerate at least two insights.

7. How do you feel about the teaching-learning experience?

SOURCE: Adapted with permission from Cruickshank (1985).   *continued*

Table 5.4 Continued

Learner Satisfaction Form for the Reflective Teaching Lesson

Name _____

1. During the lesson, how satisfied were you as a learner?

    _____ Very satisfied

    _____ Satisfied

    _____ Unsatisfied

    _____ Very unsatisfied

2. Suggest anything and everything that could have been done to increase your satisfaction with the topic, the teaching, or achievement. Be as analytical and critical (in the best sense) as you possibly can. Your responsibility is to make the teacher think deeply about teaching and learning.

— —

Learner Satisfaction Form for the Reflective Teaching Lesson

Name _____

1. During the lesson, how satisfied were you as a learner?

    _____ Very satisfied

    _____ Satisfied

    _____ Unsatisfied

    _____ Very unsatisfied

2. Suggest anything and everything that could have been done to increase your satisfaction with the topic, the teaching, or achievement. Be as analytical and critical (in the best sense) as you possibly can. Your responsibility is to make the teacher think deeply about teaching and learning.

SOURCE: Adapted with permission from Cruickshank (1985).

Contextual

Practitioners functioning at a contextual level look at alternative practices relative to the context of the situation. Analysis, clarification, and validation of principles are important in light of theory and personal values. The tasks at the contextual level support improvement of one's teaching in two ways. First, a rubric will be constructed based on values and interpretations of effective teaching. The second task allows the practitioner to use the rubric to self-evaluate and to evaluate peer microteaching.

Task 23   Effective Teaching Rubric

Topic: Practicum strategies: Microteaching

Objective: The practitioner will determine effective teaching from past experiences in schooling, then create a rubric to judge a microteaching experience.

Materials: Clear transparencies; individual copies of the Problem-Solving Scenario (Table 5.5); Problem-Solving Rubrics (Table 5.6); Definition of Rubric (Table 5.7); Sample Microteaching Rubric (Table 5.8)—optional; chart paper; markers

Time: 60 minutes

Procedure: 1. Inform practitioners that they are going to be taking a test. The test is open-ended and should be answered to the best of their abilities within a 5-minute time frame. Distribute Problem-Solving Scenario. Allow 10 minutes.

2. Using Problem-Solving Rubrics transparency, have practitioners analyze a peer's answer to the problem. Discuss how well practitioners used each of the three rubrics. Ask what might have made the task easier to do (e.g., having success indicators beforehand). Using Definition of Rubric transparency, discuss definition.

3. Knowing the criteria of success prior to microteaching is important. To develop the criteria, solicit observable indicators of effective teaching through whole-group brainstorming activity. Write list on chart paper as suggestions are given.

4. Once indicators have been listed, allow thorough discussion, making additions or deletions to the list.

5. Using a clear transparency, begin construction of the rubric. Use a 0 to 5 scale, 0 representing *no presentation* and 5 representing *top performance.* Solicit input from practitioners on key behaviors from the effective teaching list they would like their microteaching experience to be judged on. Begin with 5. List observable behaviors desired for an excellent teaching performance. An example of a completed rubric is included as an optional tool (see Table 5.6).

Task 23   Continued

6. Use the same list of effective teaching behaviors to modify for a 3 level. Then prepare the 1 level of behaviors. Indicators at level 3 should reflect moderate teaching effectiveness. Indicators at a level 1 reflect low teaching effectiveness.

7. Practitioners will use the rubric as self-evaluation and peer evaluation of microteaching experiences (such as Task 24).

Evaluation: Practitioners collaborated to produce a rubric to be used in a microteaching situation.

Debriefing: 1. On what premise were your ideas of effective reaching based?

2. How did you feel after taking the problem-solving test, then finding out the criteria?

3. What are benefits to using a rubric?

4. How might the microteaching rubric be amended?

5. What are other uses for such a rubric?

NOTE: The solution to the problem-solving scenario is that Bill and Mary are cousins.

Table 5.5 Problem-Solving Scenario

Solve the following problem by working through a problem-solving strategy. Explain the method you used to solve the problem by writing the process below the problem.

> Bill said to Tim, "You are my father." Tim said to Pat, "You are my mother." Pat said to Luke, "You are my son." Luke said to Mary, "You are my daughter." What is the relationship between Bill and Mary?

Process:

Table 5.6   Problem-Solving Rubrics

Handwriting and Neatness

5   Well-formed letters and numbers, uniform slant, no visible erasures

3   Fairly easy to read, letter formations lack consistency

1   Barely legible

Creative Labels

5   Labels are attention getting, unique, thought provoking, and imaginative

3   For the most part, representations are understandable

1   Label? What label?

Number of Words

5   More than 120 words are used in presenting solution (numbers with more than two digits constitute one word)

3   Fifty to 100 words are used in the explanation

1   One to 60 words are used (count single-digit numbers)

Table 5.7   Definition of Rubric

An assessment tool that provides standard criteria used in evaluating an action

Table 5.8 Sample Microteaching Rubric

5   Uses eye contact

Lesson has clarity (flow, accurate knowledge, clear directions)

Voice is clear, articulate, uses good grammar

Interacts with students positively

Is organized and prepared

Communicates at instructional level

Uses appropriate facial expressions and body language

Relates purpose; has closure

Lesson is varied and attention getting

Uses materials appropriately

Uses high-level questioning

Checks for understanding

Dresses professionally

Uses mobility

3   Occasionally makes eye contact

Has some flaws in lesson delivery

Poor grammar, articulation, or clarity of voice is occasionally evident

Occasionally interacts with students or has occasional negative interaction

Loses place in lesson; is somewhat unorganized

Communicates at instructional level most of lesson

Facial expressions and body language generally open and accepting

Purpose and closure weakly related

Uses attention-getting and varied strategies, sometimes ineffectively

Materials and high-level questioning used appropriately most of the time

Randomly checks for understanding

Dresses unprofessionally

Somewhat mobile in presentation

Promoting Reflective Thinking in Teachers: 44 Action Strategies
by G. L. Taggart and A. P. Wilson. Copyright © Corwin Press, 1998.   *continued*

Table 5.8   Sample Microteaching Rubric

1   Seldom uses eye contact or interacts with students

Lesson lacks clarity

Voice lacks clarity; uses poor grammar or articulation or both

Lacks organization; seems unprepared

Unsure of instructional level

Facial expression and body language are unwelcoming

Purpose is unclear or missing; closure is missing

Lesson lacks variety, is not attention getting

Materials used inappropriately; only low-level questions asked

No check for understanding

Dress is inappropriate

Presenter lacks mobility

0   No presentation

Task 24   Effective Teaching to Peers

Topic: Practicum strategies: Microteaching

Objective: The practitioner will prepare and teach a lesson to peers. Facilitator, peer, and self evaluation using a rubric will be used to assess the outcome of effective teaching.

Materials: Camcorder; VHS cassette tape; TV-VCR; microteaching rubric (from Task 23); individual copies of the Lesson Plan Format (Table 5.9)

Time: One 50-minute period; one 15-minute microteaching; one 30-minute review session

Procedure: Day 1

1. During whole-group discussion, inform practitioners that they will prepare a microteaching lesson for teaching. The practitioner first decides the topic or process to teach, then prepares a plan of the lesson. The format of the lesson is preestablished. Distribute the Lesson Plan Format. Using the Lesson Plan Format, present the overall format of the lesson. A title for the lesson will be specified, also the topic around which the lesson will be built. For example, in mathematics, the topics may pertain to the process standard of problem solving and the product standard of measurement. Specific observable performance objectives are specified on the plan. Objectives should inform the reader of what the students will learn, how they will demonstrate that learning has taken place, and by what criteria is the learning to be measured. Materials needed, time constraints, and prerequisite skills needed prior to teaching are listed. A procedure for teaching the lesson should be outlined in detail, preferably through a number system for ease of reference. Included in the teaching procedure are an introduction, a review, and a strategy development. A conclusion and evaluation of the lesson's effectiveness in producing the desired objective ends the lesson. Extensions for the student learners are drafted and resources are listed for future reference.

2. Ask for any clarifying questions. Assign a schedule of microteaching times for each practitioner.

3. The practitioner prepares and rehearses the lesson and prepares two copies of the plan, one to refer to while teaching, the other for the facilitator or peer.

continued

Task 24   Continued

Day 2

1. Practitioner teaches the lesson during a preset time period. During the teaching experience, the facilitator assesses the microteaching. Using a copy of the plan, make written comments on the effectiveness of the plan to cover the objective, its portability, and the implementation of the plan by the practitioner. Be positive regarding strategies and concepts effectively used. Note improvements needed in a constructive manner.

2. Prior to the microteaching lesson being taught, select one to four peers to perform an assessment of the practitioner teaching. Both the facilitator and peer reviewers should rate the practitioner using the rubric (Task 23) prepared by the group prior to the microteaching experience.

3. During the course of the microteaching, have the lesson videotaped by a peer or technician. The goal of videotaping is to capture the interaction of the classroom.

4. The videotaped lesson is to be reviewed by the practitioner between the teaching experience and an assigned review time with the facilitator. The practitioners use the rubric for microteaching to critique their own lessons. This review should be accomplished soon after the microteaching event.

Day 3

1. The tape and critique of the practitioner are reviewed together by the facilitator and practitioner. The practitioner explains his critique using the rubric, the video is viewed with comments made by either the practitioner or the facilitator, and the lesson plan with facilitator comments and peer critiques are given to the practitioner. It is at this time that a final grade determination is made, if needed, and goals are established for the next microteaching.

Evaluation: Practitioners planned, implemented, and evaluated a microteaching lesson.

Debriefing: 1. What parts of the microteaching experience went well? What parts needed improvement?

2. What will be a goal of improvement in your next teaching experience?

3. What are benefits to using a rubric?

4. What are benefits to performance of a microteaching lesson?

5. How is teaching to peers different than teaching to younger students?

Table 5.9 Lesson Plan Format

I.   Teacher Information

Title of lesson

Topic(s)

Student level

Objective(s)

Materials

Prerequisite skills

Time required

II. Teaching Procedures

Introduction

Review

Strategies

Conclusion

Evaluation

III. Extension

IV. Resources

Dialectical

Practicum strategies at the dialectical level deal with critical examination of underlying assumptions, norms, and rules. Social consequences are explored and choices are made after reviewing internal and external aspects of a situation. Examinations of contradictions and systematic attempts to resolve issues are characteristic of practitioner functioning in the dialectical mode. Practitioners may apply practicum strategies to improvement of teaching within an inclusionary setting and by teaching the concept of classroom management styles to peers.

Task 25 Inclusion: Teaching Effectiveness

Topic: Practicum strategies: Microteaching

Objective: The practitioner will use a 30-minute videotaped recording of their teaching to assess teaching effectiveness with special-needs children in an inclusionary setting.

Materials: Camcorder; VHS cassette tape; TV-VCR; individual copies of the Inclusion Checklist (Table 5.10); transparency of Inclusion: A Definition (Table 5.11); individual copies of the Inclusion Information Sheet (Table 5.12) and Lesson Plan Format (Table 5.9)

Time: One 50-minute period; one 15-minute to 30-minute teaching period; one 40-minute peer review session

Procedure: *Day 1*

1. Distribute Inclusion Checklist. Group practitioners by grade or age level of their field assignments. Buzz groups should have three to five practitioners per group for best results. Split larger groups. No single-practitioner groups are appropriate.

2. Use the transparency of Inclusion: A Definition, to introduce the topic, then introduce and discuss Inclusion Checklist. Allow 15 minutes for practitioners to complete them individually, then discuss items on the checklist relative to their school community. A recorder (person with most children in classroom) takes notes.

3. During whole-group discussion, have group leaders (practitioners with the most course work involving special-needs children) report findings of buzz groups. Use Inclusion Information Sheet copies to assist you in discussing the issue.

4. Practitioners will return to teams formed during buzz groups. The object is to use the Lesson Plan Format to begin planning a 15-minute to 30-minute lesson for an inclusionary classroom. Points considered in discussion should be accounted for.

5. Each team member is assigned to teach a videotaped lesson in their field setting. At least one peer will observe the teaching experience and critique the experience using the rubric from Task 23. Team members should work out a schedule for teaching and reviewing the microteaching lesson.

Task 25   Continued

Day 2

After teaching the lesson, each practitioner will view the videotape with a team member. A constructive critique of the lesson plan delivery will be made using the Inclusion Checklist as a guide.

Evaluation: Practitioners planned, implemented, and evaluated a videotaped lesson taught to students in an inclusionary classroom.

Debriefing: Practitioners will answer debriefing questions using a dialogue journal.

1. What problem did I see in my classroom regarding the inclusion of special-needs children?

2. What does inclusion mean in my classroom?

3. What solutions to the situation did I put into the lesson plan in an effort to resolve the problem?

4. What factors affected the resolution of the problem?

Table 5.10 Inclusion Checklist

Check the line at the right of each statement if you agree with the statement.

1. Do I demonstrate a genuine belief that all children are entitled to an equitable education? _____

2. Do I demonstrate a belief that all children can learn? _____

3. Is instruction individualized in my field setting for all children? _____

4. Do I alter my teaching for special-needs children? _____

5. Are resources available to meet the needs of diverse populations of students? _____

6. Do I demonstrate skill in meeting the needs of all children? _____

7. Is my field setting a supportive environment? _____

8. Are special-needs children participating in my classroom to the fullest extent possible? _____

Table 5.11   Inclusion: A Definition

A commitment to educate each child, to the maximum extent appropriate, in the school and classroom the child would normally attend

Table 5.12 Inclusion Information Sheet

The Individuals with Disabilities Education Act of 1990 (IDEA), formerly the Education for All Handicapped Children Act of 1975, stipulates that children with disabilities must be provided a free and appropriate public education in the least restrictive environment. *Least restrictive environment* generally means that children with disabilities are, to the maximum extent possible, educated with nondisabled children. Children may be placed in special classes or facilities only when the nature of their disabilities precludes satisfactory achievement in a regular classroom.

Inclusion, per se, is not mentioned in IDEA. Inclusion is a commitment to educate every child, to the maximum extent possible, in the school or classroom they would otherwise attend. Support services are brought to the child rather than moving the child to a segregated setting.

Inclusion is

All children learning in the same supportive environment

Individualization to meet the needs of all children

Equal participation by all children to the greatest extent possible

Social relationships between students with and without disabilities

Collaboration between regular and special education

Support in the classroom setting for teachers and students

All children understanding and accepting human differences

Parents participating to the fullest extent possible in the education of their children

Task 26   Effective Teaching of Peers

Topic: Practicum strategies: Microteaching

Objective: The practitioner will prepare and teach a lesson to peers. Facilitator, peer, and self evaluation using a rubric will be used to assess the outcome of effective teaching.

Materials: Camcorder; three VHS cassette tapes; three TV-VCRs; microteaching rubric (from Task 23); transparency of Definition of Classroom Management (Table 3.4); copies of Synopsis of Classroom Management Styles (Table 3.5); Lesson Plan Format (Table 5.9); clear transparencies; cards from one or two decks of playing cards

Time: One 90-minute period

Procedure: 1. Discuss with the whole group the definition of classroom management. Ask for factors that have helped to determine practitioners' management styles. List factors as presented on clear transparency.

2. Group participants into three teams by randomly distributing an ace, a king, or a queen playing card to each practitioner. Each team will become experts on either low, moderate, or high teacher control environments. Each expert group meets to assist its members in discussing the characteristics and approaches to their corresponding environmental control topic. Distribute Synopsis of Classroom Management Styles for the expert groups to use as information and to prompt discussion of possible examples. Allow about 15 minutes.

3. "Experts" will prepare a 5-minute to 10-minute lesson using the Lesson Plan Format and the microteaching rubric (from Task 23) to teach the remainder of the whole group about the level of control discussed in the team session. Allow 20 minutes.

4. Bring the whole group together for the presentation of the three lessons. Each of the three lessons will be videotaped. Select four practitioners to use the rubric to assess the presentation of each group simultaneously with the facilitator.

5. When all microteachings are completed, allow each expert group to view and critique the lesson they planned and presented, using the microteaching rubric.

6. In a whole-group situation, discuss the microteachings.

continued

Task 26   Continued

Evaluation: Practitioners planned, implemented, and evaluated a videotaped lesson to peers regarding environmental controls within a classroom.

Debriefing: 1. In which control level do you feel most comfortable? Why?

2. What was your comfort level in the peer teaching situation? Was it problematic for you?

3. How was the teaching strategy decided within the group? Was it effective?

4. How were problems resolved within the group?

5. What would have made the teaching task easier to accomplish?

6. How was reflection of the microteaching episode accomplished?

Reflective Questions

1. The use of occasional videotaping of teaching in classrooms is recommended. What benefits do you see for the practice?

2. How could reflective teaching be raised above a technical level?

3. What is the place of rubric construction in your classroom field setting?

Action Assignments

Technical

1. Compare and contrast the presentation of the cognitive and affective reflective teaching lessons taught. Discuss feelings before, during, and after teaching each lesson, attempting to determine reason for disposition. Discuss improvements made and those yet to be made. Discuss a plan for future reflective action.

2. Use a reflective teaching lesson from Cruickshank (1985) to teach a lesson in the psychomotor domain.

Contextual

1. Challenge practitioners to devise an alternative means of assessing microteaching experiences.

2. Have practitioners plan, implement, and evaluate a cooperative learning lesson plan.

Dialectical

1. Have practitioners prepare and present a lesson on an innovative strategy they would like to incorporate into the field setting. Research should be done on the strategy as well as lesson preparation. The presentation may be made to peers, administrators, and board members, or at a conference.

2. Have practitioners create and use a rubric to assess videotaped vignettes of practitioners using innovative strategies in a field setting. Discuss the vignettes, the strategy, and the rubric as an evaluation tool.

Suggestion for Success

Review rubric with practitioners after initial use and adjust if necessary.

Journaling Reflective Growth

1. Compare and contrast growth experienced before and after the practicum experience.

2. Discuss plans for future use of practicum strategies for building confidence, reflective thinking ability, and expertise in teaching.

3. Discuss changes to the practicum experiences that would be more beneficial to you.

Narrative Reflection

Narrative studies provide us with different kinds of knowledge and different ways of representing it, and studies done within the field have the potential to bring new meaning to teacher education and to the continuous experiences of change, of growth and of professional development in a teacher's life.

—*Beattie (1995)*

Chapter Objectives

The facilitator will

Assist practitioners in demonstrating proficiency in the use of the narrative strategies

Be able to assess growth in reflective thinking upon application of the strategies

Analyze personal competencies of a strategy to assist practitioners in preparing an action plan that will foster personal reflection upon return to the classroom situation

Facilitate maintenance of reflective journals to be used by practitioners for personal growth assessment and for peer assessment

The use of narrative, or story, for enhancing reflective thinking has support (Hattan & Smith, 1995; Sparks-Langer et al., 1991). Narrative writing portrays an ongoing series of events that befall one person or several people. The story line usually relates to some motive and leads to a consequence or solution. Stories can be written to describe, explain, or express. Important elements of story are the chaining of events in a logical sequence and building the events of a story around a theme, a problem, or a character, either individually or collectively. Narrative strategies used to promote reflective thinking by this author are autobiographical sketches, case studies, and the use of study circles.

Autobiographical Sketches

Autobiographical sketches are a narrative strategy used frequently by teacher educators to prompt practitioners to look into their pasts to uncover preconceived theories about teaching and learning. The perspective of education brought out in the practitioner's story line is based on beliefs, intentions, interpretations, and interactions of a lifetime. An autobiographical frame of reference assists practitioners in making sense of current experiences and in responding rationally to stimuli within those experiences. Olson (1988) maintains that practitioners' actions reflect their culture and that biographies of practitioners represent, influence, and are influenced by the cultural context in which they live. Biographies also heighten practitioners' awareness of their own learning, allowing them to reflect on changing ideas and attitudes throughout their careers (Solas, 1992). Additional benefits of using autobiographical sketches include

- Enhancement of qualitative research by opening new avenues of thought
- A vehicle for curricula and educational reform
- A foundation on which to ground educational policy and practice
- Reclamation, emancipation, and empowerment of practitioners
- Self-understanding, personal growth, and professional development

Writing autobiographies and then reflecting on the meaning and relevance of the story is a powerful tool for promoting professional growth. Holt-Reynolds (1991) writes that "biographical writing externalizes and makes accessible the interpretations . . . placed on . . . experiences; it invites them [practitioners] to reveal the underpinnings for their belief systems, goals, and arguments about 'good' teaching" (p. 16). Smith (1991) supports autobiographical reflections being used and dialogue ensured to break a cycle of teaching that may not be in keeping with current ideals of best practice.

Case Studies

Numerous studies (Bullough, 1993; Harrington, 1995; Levin, 1995) support the value of case studies in educating practitioners. A case study is a problem-centered story used to assist practitioners in focusing on problems and solutions for those situations. Because of the complexities of teaching and learning, the limited time for classroom observations, and the need to systematically look at particular episodes or aspects of teaching, case studies have become a norm in teacher education programs. Additional benefits (Boyce, King, & Harris, 1993; Kleinfeld, 1991; Shulman, 1992) to using case studies in teacher education are that they

- Bridge theory to practice
- Enable analysis of problems and development of solutions
- Help practitioners recognize the potential for multiple solutions
- Help in evaluating feasibility of alternatives and consequences of actions
- Promote critical reflection and problem solving
- Teach about dispositions and habits of teaching

The following guidelines (Silverman, Welty, & Lyon, 1992; Stivers, 1991) are used in writing case studies:

Observations

- Observe as a participant or nonparticipant
- Use narrative to capture emotional and physical environment
- Provide "thick" description of each timed observation
- Express observations with detail, not inferences

Problem Selection-Development

- Base cases on observations
- Make cases sound realistic
- Make the situation generalizable
- Interweave elements of the case to produce complex themes
- Problems should have multiple solutions
- Major practitioner should have ability to resolve the problem

Narrative Elements

- Writing is lively, fast paced, descriptive
- Limits educational jargon
- Provides rich detail
- Engages the reader with a strong opening
- Includes a climax or central incident
- Provides a gap between what is and what should be
- Presents need for a decision by major practitioner
- Organizes in a logical manner
- Avoids stereotypic and biased language
- Writes in first or third person

Study Circles

By definition, study circles are a viable strategy for enhancing reflective thinking. Brevskolan (1980) defined the aim of study circles as

> "greater understanding" or insight. Through their studies the members must be enabled to put their lives into perspective and to review their own subject in a wider context. . . . [They] must learn how to come to grips with problems and how to work out solutions in the situations that will confront them later on. (p. 13-14)

Oliver (1987) supports the use of study circles in business and education. Study circles support democratic theory, foster self-growth through education, and enhance practitioners' sense of value to become intelligent participants. Oliver adds that study circles "move us toward a more just society . . . relate ideas to action, and . . . justify our rhetoric about civic and organizational activities" (p. 145).

According to Oliver (1987), essential components of study circles are

- Reliance on dialogue
- Equality and democracy among voluntary participants
- Empowerment of participants
- Collegiality
- Self-determination
- Time for continuity and conversation
- Active participation
- Group size: 5 to 20 participants
- Use of well-grounded study materials

Reflective Activities

Technical

At a technical level, practitioners use past experiences as a frame of reference for making decisions regarding current practice. Behaviors, skills, and competencies have been developed primarily through observations during formal schooling experience. Practitioners will use existing schemata to create autobiographical sketches to access beliefs regarding teacher roles. Task 27 provides a case study for review by practitioners to augment existing schema.

Task 27   Using Case Study for Problem Resolution

Topic: Narrative reflection: Case study

Objective: The practitioner will analyze a case study to determine possible resolution to the problem posed.

Materials: Case Study: A Definition (Table 6.1); individual copies of Case Study I (Table 6.2), Case Study II (Table 6.3), and Guidelines for Writing a Case Study (Table 6.4); clear transparencies

Time: 50-minute period

Procedure: 1. In a whole-group situation, present case study definition to practitioners. Explain that practitioners will be analyzing two case studies to determine possible solutions to problems. Distribute Case Study I. Allow practitioners time to silently read the case. Solicit possible solutions from practitioners, writing them on a clear transparency. Stress that there may be multiple solutions and that all possible solutions are of value.

2. Randomly group practitioners into teams of three. Distribute Case Study II. The task for each team is to discuss all issues involved in the case to determine the best way to handle the problem. Allow 15 minutes.

3. Bring the whole group together for concluding discussion. Facilitator should solicit solutions from each team, write the solutions on a clear transparency, then facilitate analysis of solutions and bridging of ideas presented.

4. Discuss the elements of a case study by asking practitioners for observed similarities between the formats of the two cases. Distribute and discuss Guidelines for Writing a Case Study.

Evaluation: The practitioner will have determined possible solutions to a problem presented in case study format.

Debriefing: 1. How does the use of case study follow the Reflective Thinking Model (Figure 1.2)?

2. What were the bases for possible solutions presented?

3. Explain the similarities and differences in the resolution of the two problems.

4. In determining similarities and differences, what might be guidelines that may be used to write case studies?

Table 6.1   Case Study: A Definition

A problem-centered story used to assist practitioners in focusing on problems and solutions for those situations

Table 6.2   Case Study I

Ben is an 11-year-old boy in the fifth grade. He has a behavior disorder and a high anxiety level. He progresses well in Spanish and in art. However, he has a high frustration level when it comes to the main curriculum areas of science, mathematics, and social studies. He is off task most of the time and has increased difficulty in large groups. Ben takes medication before school and before he goes to physical education. Ben has frequent outbursts of "I don't understand!" followed by crying.

Ben's mother argues with him when he exhibits the yelling outburst that ends in crying at home. She never backs down or walks away from the outburst. His day at school is influenced by the way the day started out at home before he got to school. The kind of day Ben will have is evident as soon as he walks through the door.

Mr. Ortiz is frequently interrupted by Ben during mathematics, social studies, and science. "Mr. Ortiz, I don't understand what you are doing on that number line."

"Be patient, Ben, and I will explain it more in a minute."

"I don't understand!" Ben starts to cry.

Mr. Ortiz pays no attention to the crying and continues on with the lesson. The crying stops within a few seconds.

After the lesson, Mr. Ortiz has the students pick partners and goes over to his desk while the students work in groups on problems covering the concept just taught. Ben sits at a desk with two other students but doesn't work with them. "Mr. Ortiz, they won't let me work with them!"

"Ben doesn't know what to do, and we don't want him in our group," is the reply.

What should Mr. Ortiz do? Should he go at a slower pace and hold up the other students? Should he require the other two to work with Ben and help him figure out the problems? Or is there another solution?

Table 6.3 Case Study II

"Jake!"

"Andrew!"

The two captains picked their teams for recess. Over and over, names were called until there was only one boy left. As usual, it was Chris. He smiled and sat up eagerly in his chair until Luke called his name. Everyone could see that his presence made the teams uneven.

"Okay, who would like to be the umpire?" asked Ms. Smith.

Chris quickly raised his hand. No one else did.

"Chris, you can be the umpire, then."

The next week, when it was time to pick new teams, the situation was the same—Chris was the last person chosen. Again, he volunteered to be the umpire. Ms. Smith wondered why he was always picked last, but she wondered most why he kept smiling. She had never seen Chris upset about anything. He was a bolster of support to his classmates, but they gave him nothing in return. How could he continue to be so happy?

One day, another student, Cody, was having trouble with long division using decimals. When he was finished with his own work, Chris leaned over and carefully explained to Cody why the decimal needed to be moved and how the process worked. He then helped Cody until all the problems were finished and even made sure they were correct.

On another day, Ms. Smith had the students draw pictures of animals. Joe was frustrated because his bear "didn't look right." Chris turned to Joe, smiled, and said, "It's okay, Joe. Your bear doesn't have to look perfect. Just do your best."

On yet another day, Officer Martin came in to talk to the students about feelings and reactions people have to things that happen to them. One of his first examples was, How would you feel if you were standing on the playground minding your own business when you suddenly felt a rock fly by your head? While there were statements of "I'd beat 'em up!" and "I'd be mad!" Chris laughed and said, "Wow! I'd feel surprised!"

Chris's parents are presently going through a divorce. His parents won't speak to each other. The kids spend 3 days at Mom's, 4 days at Dad's, 4 days at Mom's, 3 days at Dad's, and so forth. His father is dating three women who frequently spend the night. Chris never knows who will give him breakfast in the morning at his father's house.

Right now, the turmoil in Chris's life is not evident at school. He has never had top grades, just average. He just smiles his ever-present smile and goes on. He seems very content with himself and who he is. Ms. Smith worries that he will be affected soon, and it will be worse than anyone would expect. What can she do to help Chris?

Table 6.4   Guidelines for Writing a Case Study

Observations

Observe as a participant or nonparticipant

Use narrative to capture emotional and physical environments

Provide "thick" description of each timed observation

Express observations with detail, not inferences

Problem selection-development

Base cases on observations

Make cases sound realistic

Make the situation generalizable

Interweave elements of case to produce complex themes

Problematic situations should have multiple solutions

Major practitioner should have ability to resolve the problem

Narrative elements

Writing is lively, fast-paced, descriptive

Limit educational jargon

Provide rich detail

Engage the reader with a strong opening

Include a climax or central incident

Provide a gap between what is and what should be

Present need for a decision by major practitioner

Organize in a logical manner

Avoid stereotypic and biased language

Write in first or third person

SOURCE: Adapted from Silverman et al. (1992) and Stivers (1991).

Task 28   Using Autobiographical Sketches to Evaluate Beliefs Regarding Teacher Roles

Topic: Narrative reflection: Autobiographical sketches

Objective: The practitioner will determine the role of past experiences and beliefs in determining existing perceptions of teacher roles.

Materials: Clear transparencies

Time: One 40-minute period

Procedure: 1. Allow 20 minutes for practitioners to freely write autobiographical sketches on two or three incidents remembered from formal schooling. Experiences would be more beneficial to later reflection if they were from episodes at varied time periods.

2. When practitioners have finished writing, ask for roles of teachers based on episodes remembered and explained during the free-writing exercise. A *role* is defined as a characteristic and expected social behavior of an individual. List roles as presented, on a clear transparency. Encourage practitioners to support roles mentioned by relating personal experiences from autobiographical sketches.

Discuss with practitioners the relevance of past experiences on personal perceptions.

Evaluation: Practitioners will have determined current perceptions of teacher roles through the use of autobiographical sketches.

Debriefing: 1. What value do you see in the use of autobiographical sketches?

2. In retrospect, what other incidents have helped to determine your perception of teacher roles?

3. How did you feel sharing your personal experiences with other practitioners?

4. What other areas of teaching might benefit from practitioner reflection using autobiographical sketches?

Contextual

Practitioners functioning in the contextual mode make choices within their field settings based on knowledge and value commitments. Practitioners will write a case study based on observations made in a field setting, then reflect on the problem inherent in the case. Using a study group approach, Task 30 provides an activity where practitioners will use story to analyze, clarify, and validate principles regarding effective classroom management.

Task 29   Writing a Case Study for Problem Resolution

Topic: Narrative reflection: Case study

Objective: The practitioner will observe a student in a classroom situation for 15 minutes a day on three separate days, then write a case study regarding an event indicative of the student's behavior.

Materials: Case Study: A Definition (Table 6.1); individual copies of Guidelines for Writing a Case Study (Table 6.4); clear transparencies

Time: One 50-minute period; three 15-minute observation periods; one 50-minute period

Procedure: **Day 1**

1. In a whole-group situation, present case study definition to practitioners. Explain that each practitioner will be observing a student in their respective field settings for 15 minutes on three different days to gather information for a case study of the student. Distribute Guidelines for Writing Case Studies to review the guidelines with practitioners. Practitioners are to write case studies using information from their student observations using the guidelines discussed.

Day 2

1. In a whole-group situation, discuss any experiences, positive or negative, that occurred during the observation or writing of the case studies.

2. Group practitioners into teams of three or four by having them team with individuals who have similar age or grade level field settings. No single-practitioner teams are allowed. Teams will review case studies presented.

3. The task for the practitioners will be to discuss the case studies written by each team member. Items to consider during the discussion are similarities and differences among the studies, benefits or detriments of using the guidelines, value of the case studies for future decisions in teaching, and possible solutions for each case. Teams should arbitrarily select a recorder and reporter. Allow 30 minutes.

4. In a whole-group situation, discuss the findings of each team by asking the team reporters to explain what their team learned by using the case study strategy.

continued

Task 29   Continued

Evaluation: The practitioner will have determined possible solutions to problems presented in case studies written from observations in personal field setting.

Debriefing: 1. How does the use of case study follow the Reflective Thinking Model (Figure 1.2)?

2. What were the bases for possible solutions presented?

3. What were similarities and differences among the studies?

4. What may be benefits or detriments of using the guidelines for writing case studies?

5. What value do case studies have for future decisions in teaching?

Task 30   The Three Pigs, the Wolf, and Effective Teaching

Topic: Narrative reflection: Study circles

Objective: Using *The True Story of the 3 Little Pigs!* by Scieszka as a catalyst, practitioners will delineate among ideas of effective classroom management by designating them of straw, stick, or brick value.

Materials: *The True Story of the 3 Little Pigs!* by J. Scieszka (1989); cutouts (enough for 10 of each per practitioner) of the straw, stick, and brick images (Figures 6.1A, 6.1B, 6.1C); masking tape or sticky tack; markers; labels placed on the wall about the room: "Straw," "Sticks," and "Bricks."

Time: 50 minutes

Procedure: 1. Read *The True Story of the 3 Little Pigs!* to practitioners. Briefly discuss the implications of the pigs' use of straw, sticks, and bricks to build their houses.

2. Instruct practitioners to individually analyze their own classroom management strategies or those of teachers in classrooms in which they have observed. Reflect on those strategies in terms of effectiveness in keeping students on task within the context of a given situation.

3. Using the straw, sticks, and bricks cutouts, categorize the strategies according to effectiveness: least effective (straw); moderately effective (wood), or highly effective (brick). Write the strategies on the corresponding figures and place them on the wall under the appropriate category of effectiveness. Allow 15 minutes.

4. Refer practitioners to the strategy wall. Beginning with the least effective strategies, moving to those that are moderately effective, and last to those that are highly effective, encourage practitioners to comment on why strategies were placed in a particular category.

Evaluation: Practitioners will place classroom management strategies, either practiced or observed, into categories ranging from ineffective to highly effective.

Debriefing: 1. What was one basis for your decisions on effectiveness of classroom management strategies?

2. How did discussion of the story prompt reflection on current classroom management strategies?

3. What additional topics may be reflected on using study circles?

Promoting Reflective Thinking in Teachers: 44 Action Strategies
by G. L. Taggart and A. P. Wilson. Copyright © Corwin Press, 1998.

Figure 6.1A. Material Cutouts: Straw

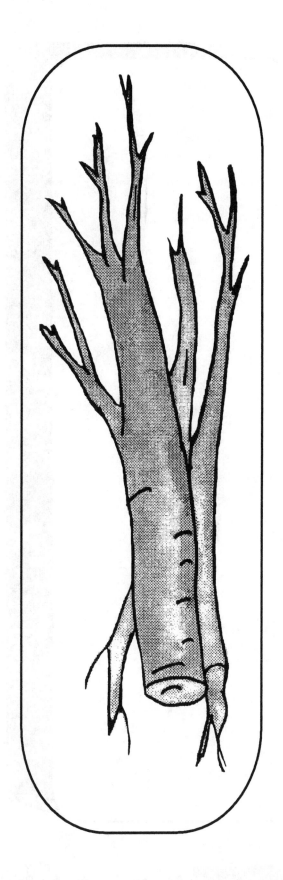

Figure 6.1B. Material Cutouts: Sticks

Figure 6.1C. Material Cutouts: Bricks

Dialectical

The implications of educational practices found in Kidder's (1989) book, *Among School Children,* are far-reaching. In Task 31, the dialectical practitioner has an opportunity to review a synopsis of a year of teaching and reflect on the relevance of similar and dissimilar instances in the practitioner's own field setting. Classroom management is again a topic of discussion in Task 32. Through autobiographical sketches, practitioners will evaluate personal beliefs and the role of those beliefs in determining classroom management strategies.

Task 31   Chew and Chat

Topic: Narrative reflection: Study circles

Objective: The practitioner will discuss episodes from *Among School Children* by Kidder (1989), reflecting on ethical judgments made by Mrs. Zajac, the book's focus teacher.

Materials: *Among School Children,* by Kidder (1989)

Time: One month preparation; 50-minute discussion

Procedure: 1. Initiate a "chew and chat" session, where practitioners may bring a meal to eat as they leisurely discuss the story of Mrs. Zajac and the ethical, moral, and sociopolitical ramifications of the issues she deals with in her fifth-grade classroom on a daily basis. The book is about a Holyoke, Massachusetts, fifth-grade teacher. Kidder provides multiple episodes from his year-long observation of Mrs. Zajac and her students.

2. Allow practitioners time to express their views on instances in the book. A free discussion of the book, initiated and supported by the practitioners, will bring the readers to points of interest as well as problems to ponder.

Evaluation: Practitioners should freely discuss the problems faced in the book and their relationships to those faced in real-life classroom situations. Occasional questioning on the part of the facilitator may be necessary to promote continuity.

Debriefing: 1. In what way were Ms. Zajac's concerns over favoritism justifiable?

2. What evidence is there that Ms. Zajac was reflective?

3. How do problems in Ms. Zajac's classroom resemble yours? How are they dissimilar?

4. What role does community play in education?

5. Describe attributes of Ms. Zajac that make her an effective teacher; an ineffective teacher. Relate instances that support your feelings.

Task 32   Using Autobiographical Sketches to Evaluate Beliefs Regarding Classroom Management Styles

Topic: Narrative reflection: Autobiographical sketches

Objective: The practitioner will determine the role of past experiences and beliefs in determining current classroom management styles.

Materials: Definition: Classroom Management (Table 3.4); individual copies of Synopsis of Classroom Management Styles (Table 3.5) and Classroom Management Approaches (Table 3.6); clear transparencies

Time: One 50-minute period

Procedure:

1. Discuss with the whole group the definition of classroom management using Definition of Classroom Management transparency. Allow 10 minutes for practitioners to individually freely write an autobiographical sketch on two or three incidents remembered dealing with classroom management. The experiences would be more beneficial to later reflection if they were from episodes at various time periods throughout formal schooling.

2. When practitioners have finished, ask for factors that have helped to determine practitioners' management styles. List factors as presented, on a clear transparency. Encourage practitioners to support factors by relating personal experiences.

3. Group participants into teams of three by having them count off to whatever number multiplied by three will equal the total number of practitioners. Use Classroom Management Approaches to briefly review various styles of classroom management. Distribute Synopsis of Classroom Management Styles to practitioners. Within each team, practitioners will review classroom environmental controls from the synopsis and determine whether they consider their personal styles to support low, moderate, or high teacher control environments. Team members should refer to the sketches written during the free-writing experience and discuss how each team member's current classroom environment correlates to incidents recorded in the sketches. Allow 30 minutes.

4. Bring the whole group together to discuss management styles, examples considered by each team, and correlations among experiences and current classroom management styles.

Promoting Reflective Thinking in Teachers: 44 Action Strategies
by G. L. Taggart and A. P. Wilson. Copyright © Corwin Press, 1998.

continued

Task 32 Continued

Evaluation: Practitioners will have determined the role of experiences, through the use of autobiographical sketches, in determining current classroom management styles.

Debriefing: 1. Explain the predominant control level. Explain possible reasons for this.

2. In which control level do you feel most comfortable? What part did past experience play in reaching this comfort level?

3. What evidence was there that the level of control changed with the context of a situation? What might advantages and disadvantages be to this change?

4. In retrospect, what other incidents have helped determine management styles?

5. What other areas of teaching might benefit from practitioner reflection using autobiographical sketches?

Reflective Questions

1. Of the three narrative strategies, which do you feel most enhances your reflective thinking ability?

2. How could the chew-and-chat idea be adapted to fit the needs of students in your field setting?

3. In what way did the autobiographical sketches cause you to remember instances from your past that you had not thought about for quite some time?

Action Assignments

Technical

1. Establish the elements of a case study by observation, then by developing a concept map of story elements relative to the use of a case study. Make comparisons and contrasts.

2. Using *Aunt Skilly and the Stranger* by Stevens (1994) as a catalyst, initiate a discussion of first impressions. Through observation and case study construction, practitioners evaluate the worth of first impressions of students in a field setting.

Contextual

1. Practitioners use Kozol's *Savage Inequalities* to reflect on alternative practices for diverse learners.

2. Practitioners use the elements of narrative to develop a personal philosophy statement on educative practice.

Dialectical

1. Practitioners will tell a story to a peer about an incident involving an ethical decision made recently in a field setting. Pairs will analyze the stories to investigate underlying values and assumptions.

2. Practitioners write an autobiographical sketch of experiences remembered throughout formal schooling. Pair practitioners and ask them to share autobiographical sketches. The readers interpret the sketches of the writers. Discussion should follow to determine how the reader's interpretation fits with that of the writer and the writer's philosophy.

Suggestion for Success

Provide sharing in a risk-free environment.

Journaling Reflective Growth

1. How did you feel about sharing life experiences? What helps to raise comfort levels?

2. How can narrative reflection be used with students in a field setting?

3. Did narrative inquiry afford changes in personal philosophy? Classroom actions?

Creating Mental Models

7

But the greatest thing by far is to be a master of the metaphor. It is the only thing that cannot be learned from others; and it is also a sign of genius because a good metaphor implies an intuitive perception of the similarity in the dissimilar.

—*Aristotle, Poetics*

Chapter Objectives

The facilitator will

- Assist practitioners in demonstrating proficiency in the use of the mental models
- Be able to assess growth in reflective thinking upon application of the strategy
- Analyze personal competence of the strategy to assist practitioners in preparing an action plan that will foster personal reflection upon return to the classroom situation
- Facilitate maintenance of reflective journals to be used by practitioners for personal growth assessment and for peer assessment

The analysis of mental models can promote reflective thinking in practitioners. Critics of teacher education programs (Elbaz, 1983; Kagan, 1992; Tabachnick & Zeichner, 1984) contend that unless mental models derived from a practitioner's past experiences are analyzed, education processes and teaching will remain virtually unchanged. Elbaz offered that images in a practitioner's existing schema often invite conformity. Prior experiences in teaching and learning serve as a filter through which the practitioner responds to new ideas. Content and experiences that confirm existing schema and images of self as teacher are accepted, whereas those that do not are rejected. Unless such images from past experiences are explicitly discussed, it is difficult to bring a practitioner's schemata in line with current educative priorities. Two strategies for bringing existing constructs of practitioners to bear are the use of metaphors and the use of repertory grids.

The Process of Using Metaphors for Reflective Thinking

The use of metaphors by facilitators of practitioners has increased in recent years. A metaphor is the transfer of meaning from one object to another on the basis of a perceived similarity. Pugh, Hicks, Davis, and Venstra (1992) state,

> Metaphorical thinking . . . entails attending to likenesses, to relationships, and to structural features in seeking what Aristotle call "similarities in dissimilarities." It involves identifying conceptual categories that may not be obvious or previously acknowledged. Metaphorical thinking cuts across subject and discipline boundaries by making knowledge in one domain a guide for comprehending knowledge in another, with some transfer of meaning taking place in both directions. Comparison is at the heart of it. . . . To be a metaphorical thinker is to be a constructive learner, one who actively builds bridges from the known to the new. (p. 4-5)

Metaphors in education stem from the schema of practitioners. The value of metaphor use is in the relationships practitioners are able to bring into a framing or reframing situation. By analyzing the relationships, schemata can be modified in one of three ways (Rumelhart & Norman, 1981):

Accretion	Gradual accumulation of information expanding existing schemata
Tuning	The refinement of new information to fit existing schemata
Restructuring	The creation of new schemata

These modifications are closely akin to Piaget's (1975) adaptations of as-similation, accommodation, and equilibrium. As practitioners acquire new insights into educational processes, modifications are attended to. The process is a valid model for restructuring new information for later retrieval.

Benefits of using metaphors in teacher education and staff development include the following (Bullough, 1994; Calderhead & Robson, 1991; Grant, 1992; Pugh et al., 1992):

- Aid in self-exploration of beliefs and values
- Help form boundaries and conditions of members
- Assist in simplifying and clarifying problems
- Help to summarize thoughts
- Enable and limit meaning
- Help develop alternative ways of looking at a topic (problem re-framing)
- Serve as bridges between a schema and new constructs
- Help form judgments about educational issues
- Assist with communication of abstract ideas
- Demonstrate underlying connections
- Gain insights into what is not yet understood

The Process of Using Repertory Grids

Kelly (1955) developed the repertory grid technique as an element of his seminal work in personal construct psychology. He posited that mental models are created from elements within individuals' views of the world and that thinking and behavior are guided by the models. Elements have relationships with one another, creating constructs. A *construct* is the way "two elements are similar and contrast with a third" (p. 61). *Repertory grids* are representations of elements and the manner in which elements are construed that reflect personal beliefs of teaching and learning and provide focus for subsequent reflection on teaching and learning (Solas, 1992).

The repertory technique has been used in teacher education. Munby (1982) studied teacher constructs to examine rationale for using certain methodologies. Olson (1988) evaluated science teachers' perspectives on student behavior. Artilles and Trent (1990) investigated preservice teachers' beliefs about effective teachers, whereas Boei, Corporaal, and van Hunen (1989) explored student teachers' notions of good teaching.

Benefits of using the repertory grid technique (Solas, 1992) include

- Linking theory with practice
- Providing a means for practitioners to analyze teaching and learning
- Increasing critical thinking regarding personal constructs
- Framing or reframing constructs that produce problems

The procedure for using the repertory technique has four steps. First, elements of a particular model are analyzed. Second, two of the elements are chosen based on a perceived difference from a third. A construct has been created. The construct should apply to all elements in the model. The dichotomy created should establish poles that house elements that are fairly equal in number. Third, the ends of the continuum are described using several descriptors, using one- or two-word phrases, if possible. Then, the element at the opposite pole continuing the dichotomy is described. Last, practitioners analyze each of the three elements of the model relative to the constructs created.

An example follows. Practitioners are to devise a repertory grid for analyzing five practitioners' classroom management styles. The practitioners become the elements, whereas classroom management is the model. Second, two practitioners are chosen based on a similarity relative to the model. Both practitioners use a teacher-centered approach to classroom management, whereas a third practitioner uses a child-centered approach.

Practitioners 1 & 2	*Practitioner*
Teacher-centered	Child-centered

Devise dichotomous descriptors for each pole. Examples may be (a) teacher determines lessons versus student determines lessons, (b) structured versus unstructured, or (c) teacher-constructed rules versus student-constructed rules. Last, practitioners analyze the two classroom management styles based on personal beliefs, values, and judgments.

Reflective Activities

Technical

Practitioners functioning at a technical level will be given the opportunity to explore teacher roles through metaphors and instructional practices by using repertory grids. The practitioners will access past experiences by using both mental models.

Task 33 Using Metaphors to Explore Teacher Roles

Topic: Mental models: Metaphors

Objective: The practitioner will, after completing Task 28, prepare a two-dimensional or three-dimensional metaphorical model of a teacher role.

Materials: Overhead transparency of teacher roles created in Task 28; Metaphor: A Definition (Table 7.1); Benefits of Using Metaphors (Table 7.2)

Time: One 10-minute period; one 50-minute period

Procedure: **Day 1**

Following completion of Task 28, use the overhead transparency developed to support the creation of a metaphorical model of a teacher role by each practitioner. In a whole-group situation, discuss with practitioners the terms *metaphor* and *benefits.* Practitioners are to select a metaphor of one role of a teacher that is particularly meaningful to them based on past and current experiences. Using the metaphor, each practitioner will create a model of the teacher role chosen. The models may be completed in two or three dimensions using any medium desired. Models will be explained on Day 2.

Day 2

1. Group practitioners in arbitrary groups of three or four. Practitioners in each team will explain their model to team members, sharing the experiences the model was based on and the relevance of the model to their current field settings. Members should also discuss the various models to determine a model that indicates the perspective of all group members. The creator of the model chosen will report to the whole group why the model was chosen as representative of the team. Allow 20 minutes.

2. In whole-group discussion, models will be shared by team members creating the models. Discuss value of metaphors.

continued

Task 33   Continued

Evaluation: The practitioner will create a model representative of a personal metaphor for teacher roles and share with team members.

Debriefing: 1. Explain how your model was illustrative of your perspective of a role of a teacher.

2. After viewing other models and listening to explanations by practitioners, explain why you accepted or rejected other models.

3. What additional metaphors for teacher roles could be added to the beginning list?

4. In what other areas of education might metaphorical analysis be of value?

5. What are alternative models for your personal metaphor of teacher roles?

Table 7.1 Metaphor: A Definition

A transfer of meaning from one object to another on the basis of a perceived similarity

Table 7.2   Benefits of Using Metaphors

- Aid in self-exploration of beliefs and values

- Help form boundaries and conditions of members

- Assist in simplifying and clarifying problems

- Help to summarize thoughts

- Enable and limit meaning

- Help develop alternative ways of looking at a topic (problem reframing)

- Serve as bridges between schema and new constructs

- Help form judgments about educational issues

- Assist with communication of abstract ideas

- Demonstrate underlying connections

- Gain insights into what is not yet understood

SOURCE: Adapted from Bullough, 1994; Calderhead & Robson, 1991; Grant, 1992; Pugh et al., 1992.

Task 34	Using Repertory Grids to Explore Instructional Practices

Topic: Mental models: Repertory grid

Objective: The practitioner will construct a repertory grid based on personal constructs dealing with instructional practices as a model.

Materials: Transparencies of the Repertory Grid: A Definition (Table 7.3) and Procedure for Creating Repertory Grids (Table 7.4); clear transparencies

Time: 50 minutes

Procedure: 1. In a whole-group situation, explain to practitioners the term *repertory grid.* Practitioners will be given 10 minutes of free-writing time to recall instructional practices remembered during their formal schooling, mentioning at least three instances with at least three former teachers.

2. Ask practitioners to relate experiences to the whole group. Write descriptors of experiences on a clear transparency.

3. Explain to practitioners that they will be using remembrances of instructional practices in constructing a repertory grid. Review procedures for constructing a repertory grid and model the following. Past teachers become the elements, whereas instructional process is the model. Use a clear transparency to illustrate the grid as the process continues. Second, two former teachers are chosen based on a similarity relative to the model. For instance, both teachers use teacher-centered processes during instruction, whereas a third teacher uses a child-centered approach.

Former Teachers 1 and 2	*Former Teacher 3*
Teacher-centered	Child-centered

Devise dichotomous descriptors for each pole. Examples may be (a) teacher determines lessons versus student determines lessons, (b) structured versus unstructured, (c) doesn't allow questions versus allows questions, or (d) lectures versus uses discovery learning. Last, practitioners analyze the two styles of instructional process based on personal beliefs, values, and judgments.

4. Instruct practitioners to use the information gleaned from their free-writing to create their repertory grid for instructional process. Monitor the construction of grids. Look for two or three practitioners willing to transpose their personal grids onto a clear transparency and share it with the whole group.

Promoting Reflective Thinking in Teachers: 44 Action Strategies
by G. L. Taggart and A. P. Wilson. Copyright © Corwin Press, 1998.   *continued*

Task 34   Continued

5. In a whole-group situation, ask targeted practitioners to share repertory grids with the group. Discuss the makeup of the grid, past experiences that led to personal constructs, and relevance to future in teaching.

Evaluation: The practitioner created a repertory grid illustrating past experiences with various instructional processes.

Debriefing: 1. How was your grid illustrative of past experiences with instructional processes?

2. On what did you base your personal constructs?

3. Of what relevance to your role as practitioner is the construct illustrative?

4. Of what relevance to your role as learner is the construct illustrative?

5. What benefit do you see to the use of repertory grids?

Table 7.3   Repertory Grid: A Definition

A representation of elements and the manner in which elements are construed that reflect personal beliefs of teaching and learning and provide focus for subsequent reflection on teaching and learning

SOURCE: Adapted from Kelly (1985). Used with permission.

Table 7.4   Procedure for Creating
                Repertory Grids

1. **Analyze** elements of a
   particular model

2. **Develop** construct: two
   elements chosen based on
   perceived difference from
   a third

3. **Describe** the dichotomous
   ends of the continuum

4. **Analyze** each of the three
   elements of the model relative
   to the constructs created

SOURCE: Adapted from Kelly (1955).

Contextual

The practitioner functioning in the contextual mode attempts to select alternatives based on contextual needs and knowledge and value commitments. Analysis, clarification, and validation of principles are used to validate the choice of the alternatives. The following two tasks will (a) assist practitioners in analyzing classroom management styles through development of metaphorical images and (b) explore traits of effective teachers by using the repertory techniques.

Task 35   Using Metaphors to Explore
Classroom Management Styles

Topic: Mental models: Metaphors

Objective: The practitioner will prepare a two-dimensional or three-dimensional model illustrating a metaphor of current preferred management style.

Materials: Transparencies of Metaphor: A Definition (Table 7.1) and Benefits of Using Metaphors (Table 7.2); clear transparencies

Time: One 15-minute period; one 50-minute period

Procedure: *Day 1*

In whole-group situation, discuss with practitioners the term *metaphor* and the benefits of the use of metaphors. Brainstorm possible metaphors for classroom management styles, writing them on a clear transparency as presented. After building a list, practitioners are to select a metaphor for a classroom management style that is particularly meaningful to them based on past and current experiences. Using the metaphor, each practitioner will create a model of the classroom management style chosen. The models may be completed in two or three dimensions using any medium desired. Models will be explained on Day 2.

Day 2

1. Group practitioners in arbitrary groups of three or four. Practitioners in each team will explain their model to team members, sharing experiences the model was based on and relevance of the model to their current field setting. Members should also discuss various models to determine a model that indicates the perspective of all group members. The creator of the model chosen will report to the practitioner group why the model was chosen as representative of the team. Allow 20 minutes.

2. In whole-group discussion, models will be shared by the team member creating the model. Discuss the value of metaphors.

Evaluation: The practitioner will create a model representative of a personal metaphor for a preferred classroom management style and share with team members.

continued

Task 35 Continued

Debriefing:
1. Explain how your model was illustrative of your perspective on classroom management.

2. After viewing other models and listening to explanations by practitioners, explain why you accepted or rejected other models.

3. What additional classroom management metaphors could be added to the beginning list?

4. In what other areas of education might metaphorical analysis be of value?

5. What are alternative models for your personal metaphor of classroom management?

Promoting Reflective Thinking in Teachers: 44 Action Strategies
by G. L. Taggart and A. P. Wilson. Copyright © Corwin Press, 1998.

Task 36 — Using Repertory Grids to Explore Practitioner Traits

Topic: Mental models: Repertory grid

Objective: The practitioner will construct a repertory grid based on personal constructs dealing with practitioner traits obtained from interviewing a teacher, a student, and a community individual.

Materials: Transparencies of Steps in Interviewing (Table 7.5) and Repertory Grid: A Definition (Table 7.3); a transparency and individual copies of Subject: Practitioner Traits (Table 7.6); clear transparencies

Time: Two 50-minute periods; one 15-minute interview period

Procedure: Day 1

1. Group practitioners into triads based on hair color. Have practitioners initially line up in order, beginning with the individual with the lightest hair color and ending with the individual with the darkest hair color. Then, section off by threes.

2. Explain to practitioners that they will be interviewing individuals to determine personal philosophies regarding practitioner traits. An *interview* is a purposeful conversation that is directed by one person to get information from the other. Using the transparency for Table 7.5, discuss Steps in Interviewing:

   A. Have prepared four to six open-ended questions on a central issue.

   B. Arrange a time with the subject, informing him or her of the purpose, length of time required, how results will be used, and so forth.

   C. Begin with small talk to develop accord with the subject.

   D. Briefly inform subject of purpose and that what is said will be treated confidentially.

   E. Ask the predetermined questions. Allow subjects time to talk freely.

   F. Interviewer may use probes such as "Could you explain that?" or ask for specific examples for the purpose of clarification.

   G. Record answers as thoroughly as possible.

   H. Interviewer should not be evaluative.

   I. When interview is completed, thank the subject for his or her time. As soon after the interview as possible, review the findings and record in a fashion that will facilitate understanding of the answers at a later date.

continued

Task 36   Continued

Practitioners will spend the remainder of the time period devising interview questions and determining interviewing strategy.

3. Instruct teams to have completed interviews prior to Day 2. One group member interviews a teacher; one, a student; the third, a community member.

Day 2

1. Discuss the definition of the repertory grid. Distribute copies of Table 7.6 (Subject: Practitioner Traits) to practitioners. Each team will create a repertory grid to organize data, feelings, and so forth. Allow 20 minutes.

2. Ask practitioners to relate their experiences to the whole group. Write descriptors of experiences on a transparency of Subject: Practitioner Traits.

3. Explain to practitioners that the whole group will be using interview details in constructing a repertory grid. Review the procedure for constructing a repertory grid by modeling the following. Interviewees become the elements, whereas practitioner traits is the model. Use a clear transparency to illustrate the grid as the process continues. Second, two interviewees are chosen based on a similarity relative to the model. For instance, both interviewees remembered a teacher trait of aloofness, whereas a third interviewee remembered a teacher trait of playing with students on the playground.

Interviewees 1 and 2	*Interviewee 3*
Aloofness	Shared experiences

Devise dichotomous descriptors for each pole. Examples may be (a) talking with another teacher on the playground versus playing with students, (b) teacher sitting at desk versus teacher moving about the room, or (c) lesson involving copying from a book versus use of manipulatives. Last, practitioners analyze the two practitioner traits based on personal beliefs, values, and judgments.

4. Discuss makeup of the grid, past experiences that led to personal constructs, and relevance to future in teaching.

continued

Task 36   Continued

Evaluation: The practitioner created a repertory grid illustrating interviewee responses to questions regarding practitioner traits.

Debriefing: 1. What were likenesses in responses by interviewees? Differences in responses?

2. Explain any unexpected responses.

3. How do responses fall in line with personnel feelings?

4. On what did interviewees base personal constructs?

5. Of what relevance to your role as practitioner are constructs, based on individuals' perceptions of practitioner traits?

6. What benefit do you see to the use of repertory grids?

Table 7.5   Steps in Interviewing

A.   Prepare four to six open-ended questions on a central issue.

B.   Arrange a time with the subject, informing them of purpose, length of time required, how results will be used, and so forth.

C.   Begin with small talk to develop accord with subject.

D.   Briefly inform subject of the purpose and that what is said will be treated confidentially.

E.   Ask the predetermined questions. Allow subjects time to talk freely.

F.   Interviewer may use probes such as "Could you explain that?" or ask for specific examples for the purpose of clarification.

G.   Record answers as thoroughly as possible.

H.   Interviewer should not be evaluative.

I.   When interview is completed, thank the subject for his or her time.

As soon after the interview as possible, review the findings and record in a fashion that will facilitate understanding of the answers at a later date.

Table 7.6   Subject: Practitioner Traits

	Teacher	Student	Community Member
Likenesses in responses			
Differences in responses			
Unexpected responses			
Responses that fall in line with personal feelings			

Dialectical

School climate is of major importance to practitioners because of moral, ethical, and sociopolitical issues. The dialectical practitioner is given opportunities in Tasks 37 and 38 to assess school climate metaphorically and by using a repertory grid.

Task 37 Using Metaphors to Explore Perceptions of School Climate

Topic: Mental models: Metaphors

Objective: The practitioner will prepare a two-dimensional or three-dimensional model illustrating a metaphor of current perception of school climate.

Materials: Transparencies of Metaphor: A Definition (Table 7.1) and Benefits of Using Metaphors (Table 7.2); clear transparencies

Time: One 15-minute period; one 50-minute period

Procedure: *Day 1*

In a whole-group situation, explain to practitioners the term *metaphor* and benefits of using metaphors. Brainstorm possible metaphors for school climate of current field setting, writing them on a clear transparency as presented. After building a list, practitioners are to select a metaphor for school climate that is particularly meaningful to them based on past and current experiences. Each practitioner will create a metaphorical model of the school climate chosen. The models may be completed in two or three dimensions using any medium desired. Models will be explained on Day 2.

Day 2

1. Group practitioners in arbitrary groups of three or four. Practitioners in each team will explain their model to team members, sharing the experiences the model was based on and the relevance of the model to their current field setting. Members should also discuss the various models to determine a model that indicates the perspective of all group members. The creator of the model chosen will report to the practitioner group why the model was chosen as representative of the team. Allow 20 minutes.

2. In whole-group discussion, models will be shared by the team member creating the model. Discuss value of metaphors.

                    continued

Task 37 Continued

Evaluation: The practitioner created a model representative of a personal metaphor for school climate and shared with team members.

Debriefing:
1. Explain how your model was illustrative of your perspective on school climate.
2. After viewing other models and listening to explanations by practitioners, explain why you accepted or rejected other models.
3. What additional school climate metaphors could be added to the beginning list?
4. In what other areas of education might metaphorical analysis be of value?
5. What are alternative models for your personal metaphor of school climate?

Task 38 — Using Repertory Grids to Explore Classroom Climate

Topic: Mental models: Repertory grid

Objective: The practitioner will construct a repertory grid based on personal constructs dealing with classroom climate as a model.

Materials: Repertory Grid: A Definition (Table 7.3); Procedure for Creating Repertory Grids (Table 7.4); clear transparencies

Time: 50 minutes

Procedure: 1. In a whole-group situation, explain to practitioners the term *repertory grid.* Practitioners will be given 15 minutes of free-writing time to recall classroom climate of current field setting and climates remembered during their formal schooling, mentioning at least two instances in each setting.

2. Ask practitioners to relate experiences to the whole group. Write descriptors of experiences on a clear transparency.

3. Explain to practitioners that they will be using information from their free-writing to construct a repertory grid. First, review the procedures for constructing a repertory grid by modeling the following: Past teachers become the elements, whereas instructional process is the model. Use a clear transparency to illustrate the grid as the process continues. Second, two former teachers are chosen based on a similarity relative to the model. For instance, both teachers use teacher-centered processes during instruction, whereas a third teacher uses a child-centered approach.

| *Former Teachers 1 and 2* | *Former Teacher 3* |
| Teacher-centered | Child-centered |

Devise dichotomous descriptors for each pole. Examples may be (a) teacher determines lessons versus student determines lessons, (b) structured versus unstructured, (c) doesn't allow questions versus allows questions, or (d) lectures versus uses discovery learning. Last, practitioners analyze the two styles of instructional process based on personal beliefs, values, and judgments.

Promoting Reflective Thinking in Teachers: 44 Action Strategies
by G. L. Taggart and A. P. Wilson. Copyright © Corwin Press, 1998.

continued

Task 38   Continued

4. Instruct practitioners to use the information gleaned from their free-writing to create their repertory grids for classroom climate. Monitor the construction of grids. Look for two or three practitioners willing to transpose their personal grids onto a clear transparency and share it with the whole group.

5. In a whole-group situation, ask targeted practitioners to share repertory grids with the group. Discuss the makeup of the grid, past experiences that led to personal constructs, and relevance to future in teaching.

Evaluation: The practitioner created a repertory grid illustrating constructs relative to classroom climate.

Debriefing: 1.   Explain the difference in ease of writing for current setting versus previous setting(s).

2.   On what did you base your personal constructs?

3.   Of what relevance to your role as practitioner is the construct illustrative?

4.   Of what relevance to your role as learner is the construct illustrative?

5.   What benefit do you see of the use of repertory grids?

Promoting Reflective Thinking in Teachers: 44 Action Strategies
by G. L. Taggart and A. P. Wilson. Copyright © Corwin Press, 1998.

Reflective Questions

1. When building a construct, why is past experience of such great importance?

2. Why are certain metaphors about education more predominant than others?

Action Assignments

Technical

1. Practitioners review newspaper articles for metaphors regarding education and effective teaching. Create a word wall of the metaphors.

2. Practitioners create a repertory grid of constructs dealing with professionalism of practitioners.

Contextual

1. Practitioners select a metaphor regarding effective teaching. Review experiences in the practitioners' pasts to analyze when accommodation of the metaphor occurred.

2. Practitioners interview administrators, asking the question, "What characteristics do you look for in a teacher candidate?" Prepare a repertory grid of responses.

Dialectical

1. Practitioners will interview community members to research mental constructs of effective teaching. After interviews, create repertory grids to reveal constructs. How do these constructs affect community support of education?

2. Practitioners will compare and contrast personal constructs based on interviews with board of education members, community members, administrators, and practitioners.

Suggestion for Success

Provide ample time for dialogue, to promote understanding of personal constructs.

Journaling Reflective Growth

1. Mental constructs are evident everywhere. What mental models are predominant in the practitioners' communities? Use newspapers and public forums as sources of information. Why are the constructs found predominant?

2. Practitioners will examine two instances in teaching where the course of action taken was a direct result of a change in beliefs based on construct analysis.

Promoting Reflective Thinking Through Action Research

Research or inquiry is a way of life, and teachers who make good decisions about curriculum are continually involved in the research process.

—*Flake, Kuhs, Donnelly, and Ebert (1995)*

Chapter Objectives

The facilitator will

Assist practitioners in demonstrating proficiency in the use of action research

Be able to assess growth in reflective thinking upon application of the strategy

Analyze personal competence of the strategy to assist practitioners in preparing an action plan that will foster personal reflection upon return to the classroom situation

Facilitate maintenance of reflective journals to be used by practitioners for personal growth assessment and for peer assessment

A *ction research* is an inquiry-oriented process of self-monitoring that allows practitioners to develop skills, assess disposition toward teaching and learning, and provide systematic experiences that foster growth in teaching and learning. It is an integral part of working in a school. Through action research, practitioners move from technical rationality (Van Manen, 1977) within the classroom to critical examination of classroom processes. Classroom processes do not fall into easily defined categories. Schön (1987) suggests that in framing a problem, teachers construct personal definitions of the problem derived from their own experiences. The practitioner moves beyond implementation of skill to critically thinking about practices and alternatives to those practices and supporting rationale. The concern no longer is unquestioned use of a textbook as a framework for teaching, for example, but one of examination of outcomes and issues of learning, such as student needs, and then finding a source or sources of information that support those outcomes and issues.

Dewey (1933) supports the idea of inquiry and experimentation. Educators of the progressive era used the scientific method to solve problems. The rationale for action research has changed little since Dewey's progressive notions of inquiry were first initiated. Practitioners carry out action research (Cochran-Smith & Lytle, 1990; Flake et al., 1995; Hagerty, Hartman, Quate, & Seger, 1994) because

- Investigations are more natural
- Findings are more credible and valid when related to practice
- Practitioners are valuable sources of knowledge regarding classroom situations
- Contemporary research lacks research in practice by practitioners
- Practitioners' research into their own practices may foster change more readily
- There is a gap between research findings and practice in the classroom
- Action research establishes a reflective, problem-solving mindset in practitioners
- Practitioners experience a chance to explore issues of interest and concern
- An opportunity exists for improved professionalism and efficacy
- Practitioners' empowerment is increased

Benefits of action research for practitioners tend to be increased thoughtfulness toward teaching; increased awareness of roles in teaching; and an increased emphasis on appropriate use of strategies, techniques, and models. In addition, practitioners' awareness of gaps between theory and practice and beliefs and practice is heightened, and a heightened awareness of student learning and thinking is fostered.

The process of action research has central characteristics (Fake et al., 1995; Gore & Zeichner, 1991; Hagerty et al., 1994; Jacob, 1995; Kemmis & McTaggart, 1988). Practitioners generally follow a process in designing and implementing action research that involves

- Identification of a problem
- Focusing on a central theme or questions
- Deciding on purpose and goals
- Selecting techniques for monitoring research
- Principles of procedures that include data gathering and analysis
- Application and implications to existing practice and further research

The process involved in action research correlates well with the reflective thinking model. The first step is to identify a problem. Identification of a problem should stem from a puzzlement or gap between what is desired and what currently exists. The central theme and subsequent question to support the research develops from considering alternative ways to frame the problem, coming to a central focus on which to base research. Purpose and goals are established supported by techniques for monitoring research. Principles of procedures are researched and decided on. These principles remind the practitioner of ethical issues surrounding the research (Gore & Zeichner, 1991). Experimentation at this level involves use of the intervention determined to resolve the problem. Procedures include gathering data by means such as field notes, interviews, sociograms, student artifacts, audio or video tapings, and through either participant or nonparticipant observations. A second and vital step in carrying out the procedure of action research is data analysis. Data analysis involves making meaning of data gathered in research. It is an ongoing and systematic way of determining the value of the intervention and monitoring the research proceedings. Final stages of the process include application considerations and implications for further action or research that may lead to a reframing of the process.

Reflective thinking activities throughout the book may serve as the foundation for action research. Information gleaned from Task 11, "Observing Effective Questioning," may provide the foundation for action research surrounding the issue of equity in questioning. Task 12, "Observing Classroom Management Styles," may open problems such as the type of feedback appropriate to facilitate learning in a low-control classroom environment. Observations, journaling, case studies, and repertory grids may serve to support and inspire the practitioner toward an inquiry approach to teaching. Gore and Zeichner (1991) maintain that action research may begin at the initial stage of teacher preparation and be sustained by the practitioner throughout the teaching career. The attempt is to construct action research projects as a natural extension of the teaching experience. "The action research provides a focus and a systematic element to their reflection in order to help the students [practitioners] work through or work within the 'problem' they experience" (p. 126).

Reflective Activities

Technical

Practitioners engaging in action research at a technical level seek to analyze and improve instruction. Task 39 provides practitioners with a forum for discussing problems within a field setting worthy of further research. The second activity in the section allows practitioners to research and reflect on a self-improvement goal following a microteaching experience prior to attempts to implement the goal.

Task 39   Preparing for Action Research: Selecting a Question

Topic: Action research

Objective: The practitioner will look at problems within a field setting, deciding on a problem of interest that may serve as a research topic.

Materials: One newsprint sheet per team of four, placed on the walls around the room; markers, transparency of Problem: A Definition (Table 8.1)

Time: 50 minutes

Procedure:
1. Group practitioners into teams of four by having them first get themselves into a line, from shortest to tallest, without conversation amongst group members. Then section off the teams of four.

2. Buzz groups will discuss the question, "What are problems observed in my field experience?" Discuss definition of problem. Allow 10 minutes at the end of which the recorders (shortest individual in each team) list situations on newsprint sheet.

3. In a whole-group discussion, investigate similarities and differences among the situations listed.

4. Allow practitioners to select one situation that would entice them to do further research, then stand by the sheet of newsprint that lists the situations. Practitioners should now be regrouped by area of interest.

5. Newly formed teams of three to five meet to determine a final and central questions to be researched. No single-practitioner teams are allowed.

6. Facilitator may choose to vary Task 40 to use as the next task toward implementing action research.

Evaluation: Practitioners will have formed a central question for research.

Debriefing:
1. What were similarities in those situations deemed problematic by practitioners? Differences?

2. Identify situations that were problematic for numerous practitioners.

3. How might the problems be categorized?

4. Is there comfort in knowing and discussing shared problems?

5. Identify situations listed beyond your control as a classroom practitioner. Why is this so?

Table 8.1   Problem: A Definition

A dilemma or puzzlement which requires action for resolution

Task 40 Research for Self-Improvement

Topic: Action research

Objective: The practitioner will select a goal following a microteaching or reflective teaching experience, research literature pertaining to the selected goal, and establish a plan to reach the goal during a subsequent microteaching experience.

Materials: Goal set following microteaching or reflective teaching experience; transparency and individual copies of Action Research Procedure (Table 8.2)

Time: 30 minutes

Procedure: 1. Once a goal has been set for subsequent microteachings or Reflective Teaching experiences, assist the practitioners in developing a plan to research means for reaching the goal. Share copies of the Action Research Procedures with practitioners. The problem, central theme, or question and the purpose and goal of the situation have already been established.

2. Using a transparency of the Action Research Procedure, outline the remaining steps in the action research process.

3. Group practitioners according to similar goals. Keep team size approximately three to five individuals. Allow no single-practitioner teams. Teams are expected to use the procedure to develop a process for reaching their teaching goals. Possible techniques may be to review literature, develop means for monitoring progress, choose criteria for determining whether or not the goal is met, and set a time line for completion.

Evaluation: Practitioners complete a plan of self-improvement toward meeting a self-imposed teaching goal.

Debriefing: 1. After discussing your goal with other practitioners, explain your level of interest.

2. What strategies for reaching the goal were discussed that may not have occurred to you before?

3. What do you perceive to be benefits of the action research process?

4. What do you perceive to be detriments to the action research process?

Table 8.2   Action Research Procedure

- Identification of a problem

- Focusing on a central theme or question

- Deciding on purpose and goals

- Selecting techniques for monitoring research

- Principles of procedures that include data gathering and analysis

- Application and implications to existing practice and further research

SOURCE: Fake et al. (1995); Gore & Zeichner (1991); Hagerty et al. (1994);
Jacob (1995); and Kemmis & McTaggart (1988).

Contextual

At the contextual level, decision making of practitioners is enhanced through action research. Practitioners with grade or building commonalities collaborate to plan a small research project. A format will be provided to the researchers that may be adapted to meet the needs of the researchers. Practitioners using Task 42 will critically examine criteria necessary for informed textbook analysis. A textbook evaluation guideline will be designed.

Task 41 Collaborative Action Research

Topic: Action research

Objective: The practitioner will collaborate with one other practitioner to research a shared problem.

Materials: Transparency of Problem: A Definition (Table 8.1); transparency and individual copies of Action Research Procedure (Table 8.2)

Time: One 50-minute period; interim research time; one 30-minute period

Procedure: Day 1

1. Group practitioners into pairs having common grade levels, school assignments, or research interests.

2. Pairs will discuss the question, "What are problems observed in my field experience?" Discuss definition of problem. Allow 10 minutes for discussion; at the end of that, each pair should have focused on one central situation that would entice them to do further research. The problem will need to be phrased into a question.

3. Distribute copies of Action Research Procedure. Outline the remaining steps in the action research process.

4. Pairs are expected to use the procedure to develop a process for researching their problem. Possible techniques may be to (a) review literature, (b) develop means for monitoring progress, (c) develop criteria for determining whether or not the goal is met and establishing a time line for completion. Provide practitioners with interim research time to carry out the procedure and analyze results.

Day 2

1. During whole-group discussion, discuss successes and problem areas in doing action research. Provide time for each pair of practitioners to share their research with fellow practitioners. Make the environment relaxing and risk free. You may want to set chairs in a circular fashion.

Evaluation: Practitioners complete a research plan to investigate a common problem.

Debriefing: 1. Identify common successes and problems found in action research.

2. Explain the favorability or unfavorability regarding collaboration on a research project.

3. What do you perceive to be benefits of the action research process?

4. What do you perceive to be detriments to the action research process?

5. How might you use action research to support your teaching practice in the future?

Task 42   Textbook Analysis

Topic: Action research

Objective: The practitioner will review a textbook series, discuss textbook selection criteria, then collaborate to produce a textbook analysis form.

Materials: One to three complete textbook series covering the grade and age levels in field settings of practitioners; chart paper; individual copies of Action Research Procedure (Table 8.2); Fry's Readability Graph (Figure 8.1); clear transparencies; Sample Textbook Analysis Form (Form 8.1)—optional

Time: Three 30-minute periods

Procedure: Day 1

1. Group practitioners into teams of three to five by grade or age level taught. Allow no single-practitioner teams.

2. In the first 50-minute period, allow teams to review textbook series. A central question to be asked is, "What characteristics of a textbook are important to a practitioner for effective teaching?" Each team selects a recorder, a reporter, and a materials person. The recorder writes down pertinent information to complete the task. The reporter will report as information is requested. And the materials person is responsible for obtaining and organizing materials. A typist may also be selected for typing a final product.

Day 2

1. During whole-group discussion, reporters from teams formed during Day 1 will present characteristics discussed in the team meetings. Facilitator will write characteristics on chart paper. When the list is complete, ask teams what categories can be formed by combining some of the characteristics. Possible categories are Teacher Edition, Readability, Construction, and so forth. Instruct practitioners in use of Fry's Readability Graph if it is new to them.

2. Instruct practitioners to devise a textbook analysis format that may be used to evaluate textbooks for their classroom. Using a clear transparency, list special considerations suggested by practitioners that have not already been discussed. It is at the facilitator's discretion whether or not to distribute the sample Textbook Analysis Form at this time. Allow practitioners the remainder of the time to prepare prototypes. The prototypes should be typed and copied for each team member by Day 3.

   continued

Task 42   Continued

Day 3

Prototypes will be used during this 50-minute time period. Group practitioners in original teams from Day 1. Provide practitioners with textbook series to review using the prototype instrument. The recorder should write observations made by team members during the review process. Allow 40 minutes.

Evaluation: Practitioners developed a textbook analysis document to meet the needs of textbook evaluation as a problem.

Debriefing: 1. Identify the characteristics of textbooks that you did not previously know existed.

2. Explain how you arrive at a procedure for completing this task.

3. How might this task have been completed differently if the facilitator had given teams a sample document prior to creation of the prototype? (optional)

4. What are implications of your research?

5. What other research applications may be linked to this type of activity?

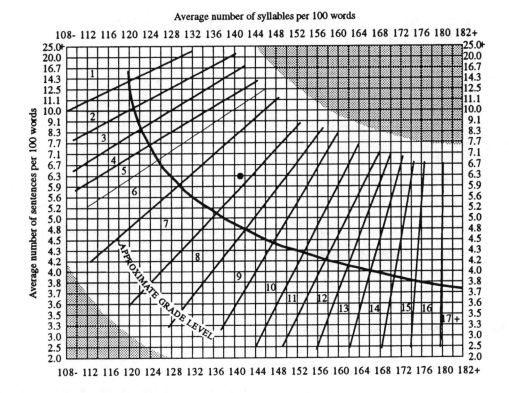

Average number of syllables per 100 words

Expanded Directions for Working Readability Graph

1. Randomly select three (3) sample passages and count out exactly 100 words each, beginning with the beginning of a sentence. Do count proper nouns, initializations, and numerals.

2. Count the number of sentences in the hundred words, estimating length of the fraction of the last sentence to the nearest one tenth.

3. Count the total number of syllables in the 100-word passage. If you don't have a hand counter available, an easy way is to simply put a mark above every sylla- ble over one in each word; then when you get to the end of the passage, count the number of marks and add 100.

4. Enter graph with average sentence length and average number of syllables; plot dot where the two lines intersect. Area where dot is plotted will give you the ap- proximate grade level.

5. If a great deal of variability is found in syllable count or sentence count, putting more samples into the average is desirable.

Figure 8.1. Fry's Readability Graph

SOURCE: Fry (1977).

Form 8.1   Sample Textbook Analysis Form

General Information

A. Title of textbook _____

B. Author(s) _____

C. Publisher _____

D. Date of copyright _____

E. Cost _____

F. Publisher or author's suggested readability level _____

G. Readability level _____

Directions for Completing This Form

A. Rate each question using the scale below.

B. Give each section its own average score determined by aspects you feel are relevant. Comment on these aspects at the end of the evaluation.

C. Record the average scores from each section on the chart below.

D. Find the mean of the Section Averages to determine overall rating of the text.

I.	_____	Physical features	V.	_____	Content
II.	_____	Readability	VI.	_____	Book parts
III.	_____	Graphics	VII.	_____	Skills and activities
IV.	_____	Authorship	VIII.	_____	Manual

Total score   _____

Total average   _____

continued

Form 8.1 Continued

Rate the following questions according to the following scale by circling your response:

> 3 = Good
> 2 = Average
> 1 = Poor
> NA = Not Applicable

I. Physical features (Section average_____)

    A. 3 2 1 NA   Appealing size and appearance

    B. 3 2 1 NA   Durability

II. Readability (Section average_____)

    A. 3 2 1 NA   Reading level versus grade level

    B. 3 2 1 NA   Presentation of material

    C. 3 2 1 NA   Vocabulary growth (use of new vocabulary)

III. Graphics (Section average_____)

    A. 3 2 1 NA   Well-chosen

    B. 3 2 1 NA   Explanation close to graphic

    C. 3 2 1 NA   Current

    D. 3 2 1 NA   Aesthetic value

    E. 3 2 1 NA   Maps

IV. Authorship (Section average_____)

    A. 3 2 1 NA   Expertise

    B. 3 2 1 NA   Experience in classroom

    C. 3 2 1 NA   Style of writing

V. Content (Section average_____)

    A. 3 2 1 NA   Promotes cognitive growth

    B. 3 2 1 NA   Reflects experiences of today's children

    C. 3 2 1 NA   Free of stereotyping

    D. 3 2 1 NA   Objectives indicated and assessed

continued

Form 8.1 Continued

VI. Book parts (Section average_____)

    A. 3 2 1   NA   Additional suggested reading lists

    B. 3 2 1   NA   Supplementary resource list

    C. 3 2 1   NA   Comprehensive index

    D. 3 2 1   NA   Glossary

VII. Skills & activities (Section average_____)

    A. 3 2 1   NA   Meets state and district objectives

    B. 3 2 1   NA   Review practices

    C. 3 2 1   NA   Various levels of activities

    D. 3 2 1   NA   Various types of activities

    E. 3 2 1   NA   Assessment fits activities

VIII. Manual (Section average_____)

    A. 3 2 1   NA   Clear, detailed lessons

    B. 3 2 1   NA   Durability

    C. 3 2 1   NA   Practical activities and suggestions

    D. 3 2 1   NA   Enrichment and reteaching activities

Summary Statements

A. As a teacher, explain your degree of comfort with this material.

B. As a member of the community, parent, or administrator, explain whether or not you would be in favor of this material.

C. Write a composite statement listing strengths and weaknesses of the text.

D. Explain the appropriate use of this text series for diverse populations of students.

E. Provide any additional comments, suggestions, or ideas that you feel are relevant to the adoption of this text.

            Decision: Adopt   _____

                           Reject   _____

                           Evaluator _____

                           Date   _____

Dialectical

Practitioners functioning in the dialectical mode are aware of social, political, and ethical issues in school cultures. Action research is carried out to seek change based on ethical, moral, or sociopolitical issues of situations that are problematic to the practitioners. Task 44 provides the practitioners an opportunity to research the same issues that are problematic to the practitioner relative to parental or community involvement.

Task 43 Action Research: Ethical, Moral, or Sociopolitical Issues

Topic: Action research

Objective: The practitioner will collaborate with one other practitioner to research a shared problem dealing with an ethical, moral, or sociopolitical issue.

Materials: Transparency of Problem: A Definition (Table 8.1); transparency and individual copies of Action Research Procedure (Table 8.2)

Time: One 50-minute period; interim research time; one 30-minute period

Procedure: Day 1

1. Group practitioners into pairs having common grade levels, school assignments, or research interests.

2. Pairs will discuss the question, "What are problems dealing with moral, ethical, or sociopolitical issues observed in my field experience?" Discuss definition of a problem. Allow 10 minutes for discussion; at the end of that, each pair should have focused on one central situation that would entice them to do further research. The problem will need to be phrased into a question.

3. Distribute copies of Action Research Procedure. Outline the remaining steps in the action research process.

4. Pairs are expected to use the procedure to develop a process for researching their problems. Possible techniques may be to review literature, develop means for monitoring progress, and determine criteria for determining whether or not the goal is met and a time line for completion. Provide practitioners with interim research time to carry out the procedure and analyze results.

Day 2

1. During whole-group discussion, discuss successes and problem areas in doing action research. Provide time for each pair of practitioners to share their research with fellow practitioners. Make the environment relaxing and risk free. You may want to set chairs in a circular fashion.

                      continued

![Task 43] **Continued**

Evaluation: Practitioners complete a research plan to investigate a common problem.

Debriefing:
1. Identify the common successes and problems found in action research.
2. Was collaborating on a research project favorable to you?
3. What do you perceive to be benefits of the action research process?
4. What do you perceive to be detriments to the action research process?
5. How might you use action research to support your teaching practice in the future?
6. What was your comfort level in dealing with issues relating to your values and beliefs?

Task 44   Action Research: Parent and Community Involvement

Topic: Action research

Objective: The practitioner will collaborate with one other practitioner to research a shared problem related to parent and community involvement.

Materials: Transparency of Problem: A Definition (Table 8.1); transparency and individual copies of Action Research Procedure (Table 8.2)

Time: One 50-minute period; interim research time; one 30-minute period

Procedure: *Day 1*

1. Group practitioners into pairs having common grade levels, school assignments, or research interests.

2. Pairs will discuss the question, "What are problems observed in my field experience that deal with parent or community involvement?" Discuss definition of a problem. Allow 10 minutes for discussion; at the end of that, each pair should have focused on one central situation that would entice them to do further research. The problem will need to be phrased into a question.

3. Distribute copies of the Action Research Procedure. Outline the remaining steps in the action research process.

4. Pairs are expected to use the procedure to develop a process for researching their problems. Possible techniques may be to review literature, develop means for monitoring progress, and set criteria for determining whether or not the goal is met and a time line for completion. Provide practitioners with interim research time to carry out the procedure and analyze results.

Day 2

During whole-group discussion, discuss successes and problem areas in doing action research. Provide time for each pair of practitioners to share their research with fellow practitioners. Make the environment relaxing and risk free. You may want to set chairs in a circular fashion.

                    continued

Task 44   Continued

Evaluation: Practitioners complete a research plan to investigate a common problem.

Debriefing:
1. Identify common successes and problems found in action research.

2. Was collaborating on a research project favorable to you? Why? Why not?

3. What do you perceive to be benefits of the action research process?

4. What do you perceive to be detriments to the action research process?

5. How might you use action research to support your teaching practice in the future?

6. What other situations regarding parent or community involvement would interest you in doing additional action research?

Reflective Questions

1. What characteristics of action research would make you want to use the strategy? Not want to use the strategy?

2. How can action research improve student achievement?

Action Assignments

Technical

1. Practitioners review educational journal articles for innovative strategies for classroom instruction. They will then analyze an article's contents, reacting to the article and strategy; relating the relevance of the strategy to current and future field settings and responding to the responsibility toward using the strategy in practice.

2. Practitioners will adopt the perspective of an educational theorist, presenting a rationale for his or her actions and philosophy through a narrative format or by role-playing.

Contextual

1. Practitioners will review types of research engaged in to this point in their careers. Through buzz groups, analyze how action research within their own field setting will be alike and dissimilar to past experiences in research.

2. Practitioners will review with a peer existing tests taken by students in an effort to ascertain the validity of the tests and the relevance of the tests in producing the type of results and information desired of the instrument.

Dialectical

1. Practitioners will research, through interview and document discovery, the views of the media on education. Of particular interest may be media analyses of test results, reactions to unethical teachers, or issues regarding funding. Of interest may be the impact on public opinion of education supported by the viewpoints of the media.

2. Practitioners will research student attitudes, through observation and survey, toward issues such as use of manipulatives, silent sustained reading, or discovery learning in science.

Suggestion for Success

Provide sufficient time to plan, implement, and discuss research.

Journaling Reflective Growth

1. Assuming action research caused you to look at problems in a different light, what made this possible? If it was not possible, what caused this to be so?

2. Reflect on cognitive growth regarding problems researched. Has there also been social or emotional growth? Reflective growth? Explain.

References

Aronson, E., Blaney, N., Stephan, D., Sikes, J., & Snapp, M. (1978). *The jig-saw classroom.* Beverly Hills, CA: Sage.

Artilles, A. J., & Trent, S. C. (1990). *Characteristics and constructs: pro-spective teachers' descriptions of effective teachers.* (ERIC Document Reproduction Service No. ED 340 691)

Bandura, A. (1968). *Social foundations of thought and action: A social cognitive theory.* Englewood Cliffs, NJ: Prentice Hall.

Beattie, M. (1995). New prospects for teacher education: Narrative ways of knowing teaching and teacher learning. *Educational Research, 37*(1), 53-70.

Bigge, M. L., & Shermis, S. S. (1992). *Learning theories for teachers* (5th ed.). New York: HarperCollins.

Boei, F., Corporaal, A. H., & van Hunen, W. H. (1989). Describing teacher cognitions with the Repgrid: Some methodological reflections and re-search findings. In J. Lowyck & C. M. Clark (Eds.), *Teacher thinking and professional action.* Leuven, Belgium: Leuvenarolyn University Press.

Bolin, F. S. (1988). Helping student teachers think about teaching. *Journal of Teacher Education, 39*(2), 48-54.

Borich, G. D. (1994). *Observation skills for effective teaching* (2nd ed.). New York: Macmillan.

Boyce, B. A., King, V., & Harris, B. (1993). *The case study approach for pedagogists* (Report No. SP 034 505). Washington, DC: American Alli-ance for Health, Physical Education, Recreation and Dance. (ERIC Document Reproduction Service No. ED 361 286)

Brevskolan. (1980). *The study circle: A brief introduction.* Stockholm: Author.

Brooks, J. G., & Brooks, M. G. (1993). *In search of understanding: The case for constructivist classrooms.* Alexandria, VA: Association for Supervi-sion and Curriculum Development.

Browder, D. M., Schoen, S. F., Lentz, F. E. (1986-87). Learning to learn through observation. *Journal of Special Education, 20*(4), 447-460.

Brubacher, J. W., Case, C. W., & Reagan, T. G. (1994). *Becoming a reflec-tive educator: How to build a culture of inquiry in the schools.* Thou-sand Oaks, CA: Corwin.

Bullough, R. V. (1993). Case records as personal teaching texts for study in preservice teacher education. *Teaching & Teacher Education, 9*(4), 385-396.

Bullough, R. V. (1994). Analyzing personal teaching metaphors in preservice teacher education as a means for encouraging professional development. *American Educational Research Journal, 31*(1), 197-224.

Bullough, R. V., Jr. (1991). Exploring personal teaching metaphors in preservice teacher education. *Journal of Teacher Education, 42*(1), 43-51.

Burden, P. R. (1995). *Classroom management and discipline.* White Plains, NY: Longman.

Calderhead, J., & Robson, M. (1991). Images of teaching: Student teachers' early conceptions of classroom practice. *Teaching and Teacher Education, 7,* 1-8.

Clarke, A. (1995). Professional development in practicum settings: Reflective practice under scrutiny. *Teaching & Teacher Education, 11*(3), 243-261.

Clift, R. T., Houston, W. R., & Pugach, M. C. (Eds.). (1990). *Encouraging reflective practice in education: An analysis of issues and programs.* New York: Teachers College Press.

Cochran-Smith, M., & Lytle, S. L. (1990). Research on teaching and teacher research: The issues that divide. *Educational Researcher, 19*(2), 2-11.

Connelly, F. M., & Clandinin, D. J. (1986). On narrative method, personal philosophy, and narrative unities in the story of teaching. *Journal of Research in Science Teaching, 23*(4), 293-310.

Copeland, W. D., Birmingham, C., De La Cruz, E., & Lewin, B. (1993). The reflective practitioner in teaching: Toward a research agenda. *Teaching & Teacher Education, 9*(4), 347-359.

Cruickshank, D. R. (1985). Uses and benefits of reflective teaching. *Phi Delta Kappan, 66*(10), 704-706.

Cruickshank, D. R. (1987). *Reflective teaching: The preparation of students of teaching.* Reston, VA: Association of Teacher Educators.

Cruickshank, D. R., Kennedy, J. J., Williams, E. J., Holton, J., & Fay, D. E. (1981). Evaluation of reflective teaching outcomes. *Journal of Educational Research, 75*(1), 26-31.

Dewey, J. (1933). *How we think.* Boston: D. C. Heath.

Driekurs, R., Grunwald, B. B., & Pepper, F. C. (1982). *Maintaining sanity in the classroom: Classroom management techniques* (2nd ed.). New York: Harper & Row.

Eby, J. W., & Kujawa, E. (1994). *Reflective planning, teaching, and evaluation: K-12.* New York: Macmillan.

Elbaz, F. (1983). *Thinker thinking: A study of practical knowledge.* London: Croom Helm.

Flake, C. L., Kuhs, T., Donnelly, A., & Ebert, C. (1995). Reinventing the role of teacher: Teacher as researcher. *Phi Delta Kappan, 76*(5), 405-407.

Fosnot, C. T. (1989). *Inquiring teachers, inquiring learners: A constructivist approach for teaching.* New York: Teachers College Press.

Fry, E. (1977). Fry's readability graph: Clarifications, validity, and extension to level 17. *Journal of Reading, 21,* 242-252.

Fullan, M. (1991). *The new meaning of educational change.* New York: Teachers College Press.

Garman, N.B. (1986). Reflection, the heart of clinical supervision: A modern rationale for professional practice. *Journal of Curriculum and Supervisor, 2*(1), 1-24.

Glasser, W. (1969). *Schools without failure.* New York: Harper & Row.

Glasser, W. (1992). *The quality school: Managing students without coercion* (2nd ed.). New York: HarperPerennial.

Glasser, W. (1993). *The quality school teacher.* New York: HarperPerennial.

Gore, J. M. (1987). Potpourri: Reflecting on reflective teaching. *Journal of Teacher Education, 36,* 33-39.

Gore, J. M., & Zeichner, K. M. (1991). Action research and reflective teaching in preservice teacher education: A case study from the United States. *Teaching & Teacher Education, 7(2),* 119-136.

Grant, G. E. (1992). The sources of structural metaphors in teacher knowledge: Three cases. *Teaching and Teacher Education, 8*(5 & 6), 433-440.

Grimmett, P. P., MacKinnon, A. M., Erickson, G. L., & Riecken, T. J. (1990). Reflective practice in teacher education. In R. T. Clift, W. R. Houston, & M. C. Pugach (Eds.), *Encouraging reflective practice in education: An analysis of issues and programs* (pp. 20-38). New York: Teachers College Press.

Hagerty, P., Hartman, K., Quate, S., & Seger, D. (1994). *Becoming a teacher researcher: What every classroom teacher should know.* Unpublished manuscript.

Harrington, H. L. (1995). Fostering reasoned decisions: Case-based pedagogy and the professional development of teacher. *Teaching & Teacher Education, 11*(3), 203-214.

Harrington-Macklin, D. (1994). *The team building tool kit—Tips, tactics, and rules for effective workplace teams.* New York: AMACOM.

Hattan, N., & Smith, D. (1994). *Facilitating reflection: Issues and research* (Report No. SP 035 487). Brisbane, Queensland, Australia: Australian Teacher Education Association. (ERIC Document Reproduction Service No. ED 375 110)

Hattan, N., & Smith, D. (1995). Reflection in teacher education: Towards definition and implementation. *Teaching and Teacher Education, 11*(1), 33-49.

Heathcote, D. (1980). *Drama as context.* Aberdeen, Scotland: Aberdeen University Press; The National Association for the Teaching of English.

Holt-Reynolds, D. (1991). *The dialogues of teacher education: Entering and influencing preservice teachers' internal conversations* (Report

No. 91-4). Washington, DC: Office of Educational Research and Improvement. (ERIC Document Reproduction Service No. ED 337 459)

Houston, W. R., & Clift, R. T. (1990). The potential for research contributions to reflective practice. In R. T. Clift, W. R. Houston, & M. C. Pugach (Eds.), *Encouraging reflective practice in education: An analysis of issues and programs* (pp. 208-224). New York: Teachers College Press.

Jacob, E. (1995). Reflective practice and anthropology in culturally diverse classrooms. *The Elementary School Journal, 95*(5), 451-463.

Johnson, D. W., Johnson, R. T., & Holubec, E. J. (1991). *Cooperation in the classroom* (Rev. ed.). Edina, MN: Interaction.

Joyce, B., & Showers, B. (1995). *Student achievement through staff development: Fundamentals of school renewal* (2nd ed.). White Plains, NY: Longman.

Kagan, D. M. (1992). Professional growth among preservice and beginning teachers. *Review of Educational Research, 62*(2), 129-169.

Kelly, G. (1955). *The psychology of personal constructs: A theory of personality* (Vol. 1). New York: Norton.

Kemmis, S., & McTaggart, R. (1988). *The action research planner* (3rd ed.). Geelong, Australia: Deakin University Press.

Kidder, T. (1989). *Among school children.* New York: Avon.

Kirby, P., & Teddlie, C. (1989). Development of the reflective teaching instrument. *Journal of Research and Development in Education, 22*(4), 45-51.

Kleinfeld, J. (1991). *Wrestling with the angel: What student teachers learn from writing cases* (Report No. SP 033 462). Chicago: American Educational Research Association. (ERIC Document Reproduction Service No. ED 347 123)

Knowles, M. (1990). *The adult learner: A neglected species* (4th ed.). Houston, TX: Gulf.

Korthagen, F. A. J. (1985). Reflective teaching and preservice teacher education in the Netherlands. *Journal of Teacher Education, 36,* 11-15.

Korthagen, F. A. J., & Wubbels, T. (1991, April). *Characteristics of reflective practitioners: Towards an operationalization of the concept of reflection.* Paper presented at the Annual Meeting of the AERA, Chicago, IL.

Kounin, J. S. (1970). *Discipline and group management in classrooms.* New York: Holt, Rinehart & Winston.

Lasley, T. J. (1992). Promoting teacher reflection. *Journal of Staff Development, 13*(1), 24-29.

Levin, B. B. (1995). Using the case method in teacher education: The role of discussion and experience in teachers' thinking about cases. *Teaching & Teacher Education, 11*(1), 63-79.

Marshall, C., & Rossman, G. B. (1995). *Designing qualitative research* (2nd ed.). Thousand Oaks, CA: Sage.

McHaney, J. H., & Impey, W. D. (1992). *Strategies for analyzing and evaluating teaching effectiveness using a clinical supervision model* (Report No. TM 019 556). Knoxville, TN: Mid-South Educational Research Association. (ERIC Document Reproduction Service No. ED 354 268)

Munby, H. (1982). The place of teachers' beliefs in research on teacher thinking and decision making, and an alternative methodology. *Instructional Science, 11*, 201-225.

Munby, H., & Russell, T. (1989). *Metaphor in the study of teachers' professional language.* Paper presented at the annual meeting of the American Educational Research Association, San Francisco, CA.

Nelsen, J. (1987). *Positive discipline* (2nd ed.). New York: Ballantine.

Noordhoff, K., & Kleinfeld, J. (1990). Shaping the rhetoric of reflection for multicultural settings. In R. T. Clift, W. R. Houston, & M. C. Pugach (Eds.), *Encouraging reflective practice in education: An analysis of issues and programs* (pp. 186-207). New York: Teachers College Press.

Norton, J. L. (1994, February). *Creative thinking and locus of control as predictors of reflective thinking in preservice teachers.* Paper presented at the 74th Annual Meeting of the Association of Teacher Educators, Atlanta, GA.

Oliver, L. P. (1987). *Study circles: Coming together for personal growth and social change.* Washington, DC: Seven Locks.

Olson, J. (1988). Making sense of teaching: Cognition vs. culture. *Journal of Curriculum Studies, 12,*1-11.

Orlich, D. C., Harder, R. J., Callahan, R. C., Kauchak, D. P., & Gibson, H. W. (1994). *Teaching strategies: A guide to better instruction* (4th ed.). Lexington, MA: D. C. Heath.

Piaget, J. (1975). *The development of thought: Equilibration of cognitive structures.* New York: Viking.

Posner, G. J. (1996). *Field experience: A guide to reflective teaching* (4th ed.). White Plains, NY: Longman.

Pugach, M. C., & Johnson, L. J. (1990). Developing reflective practice through structured dialogue. In R. T. Clift, W. R. Houston, & M. C. Pugach (Eds.), *Encouraging reflective practice in education: An analysis of issues and programs* (pp. 186-207). New York: Teachers College Press.

Pugh, S. L., Hicks, J. W., Davis, M., & Venstra, T. (1992). *Bridging: A teacher's guide to metaphorical thinking.* Urbana, IL: National Council of Teachers of English.

Ross, D. D. (1989). First steps in developing a reflective approach. *Journal of Teacher Education, 40*(1), 22-30.

Ross, D. D. (1990). Programmatic structures for the preparation of reflective teachers. In R. T. Clift, W. R. Houston, & M. C. Pugach (Eds.), *Encouraging reflective practice in education: An analysis of issues and programs* (pp. 97-118). New York: Teachers College Press.

Ross, E. W., & Hannay, L. M. (1986). Towards a critical theory of reflective inquiry. *Journal of Teacher Education, 37*, 9-15.

Rumelhart, D. E., & Norman, D. A. (1981). Accretion, tuning, and restructuring: Three modes of learning. In J. W. Cotton & R. Klatzky (Eds.), *Semantic factors in cognition* (pp. 37-60). Hillsdale, NJ: Erlbaum.

Schön, D. A. (1983). *Educating the reflective practitioner: Toward a new design for teaching and learning in the professions.* San Francisco: Jossey-Bass.

Schroeder, M. L. (1996). Lesson design and reflection. *Mathematics Teaching in the Middle School, 1*(18), 648-652.

Scieszka, J. (1989). *The true story of the 3 little pigs!* New York: Viking Penguin.

Shulman, J. (Ed.). (1992). *Case method in teacher education.* New York: Teachers College Press.

Silverman, R., Welty, W. M., & Lyon, S. (1992). *Case studies for teacher problem solving.* New York: McGraw-Hill.

Simmons, J. M., & Sparks, G. M. (1987). *The need for a new model of teacher supervision & evaluation: The implications of identifying reflection as an explicit goal of teacher education programs.* Houston: OERI Conference on Teacher Reflection.

Slavin, R. E. (1983). *Cooperative learning.* New York: Longman.

Smith, R. W. (1991). *Obstacles to student teacher reflection: The role of prior school experience as a barrier to teacher development* (Report No. SP 033 243). Chicago: American Educational Research Association. (ERIC Document Reproduction Service No. ED 336 352)

Solas, J. (1992). Investigating teacher and student thinking about the process of teaching and learning using autobiography and repertory grid. *Review of Educational Research, 62*(2), 205-225.

Sparks-Langer, G. M., Colton, A. B., Pasch, M., & Starko, A. (1991). *Promoting cognitive, critical, and narrative reflection* (Report No. SP 033 326). Chicago: American Educational Research Association. (ERIC Document Reproduction Service No. ED 337 435)

Staton, J. (1987). The power of responding in dialogue journals. In T. Fulwiler (Ed.), *The journal book.* Portsmouth, NH: Heinemann.

Stevens, K. (1994). *Aunt Skilly and the stranger.* New York: Ticknor & Fields.

Stivers, J. (1991). *An introduction to case use in teacher education* (Report No. SP 034 030). New York: Confederated Organizations of Colleges for Teacher Education and New York State Association of Teacher Educators. (ERIC Document Reproduction Service No. ED 348 366)

Tabachnick, B. R., & Zeichner, K. (1984). The impact of the student teaching experience on the development of teacher perspectives. *Journal of Teacher Education, 35,* 28-36.

Taggart, G. L., Phifer, S. J., Nixon, J. A., & Wood, M. (Eds.). *Rubrics: A handbook for construction and use.* Lancaster, PA: Technomic.

Valli, L. (1990). *Teaching as moral reflection: Thoughts on the liberal preparation of teachers* (Report No. SP 033 712). Milwaukee, WI: Association of Independent Liberal Arts Colleges for Teacher Education. (ERIC Document Reproduction Service No. ED 344 853)

Van Manen, M. (1977). Linking ways of knowing with ways of being practical. *Curriculum Inquiry, 6*(3), 205-228.

Wubbels, T., & Korthagen, F. A. J. (1990). The effects of a pre-service teacher education program for the preparation of reflective teachers. *Journal of Education for Teaching, 16*(1), 29-43.

Yinger, R., & Clark, C. (1981). *Reflective journal writing: Theory and practice* (Occasional Paper No. 50). East Lansing, MI: Institute for Research and Teaching.

Zeichner, K. M. (1983). Alternative paradigms of teacher education. *Journal of Teacher Education, 34*(3), 3-9.

Zeichner, K. M. (1987). Preparing reflective teachers: An overview of instructional strategies which have been employed in preservice teacher education. *International Journal of Educational Research, 11*(5), 565-576.

Zeichner, K. M., & Liston, D. P. (1987). Teaching student teachers to reflect. *Harvard Educational Review, 57,* 23-48.

Zinsser, W. (1988). *Writing to learn: How to write and think clearly about any subject at all.* New York: Harper & Row.